Lancashire Nicknames and Sayings

by
Bob Dobson

DALESMAN BOOKS
1977

£1

The Dalesman Publishing Company Ltd.,
Clapham (via Lancaster), North Yorkshire.

First published 1973

Second edition 1977

© Bob Dobson 1973, 1977

ISBN: 0 85206 406 3

I dedicate this book to the glorious memory of Superintendent Gerry Richardson, who was killed on duty on Monday, 23rd August, 1971, at Blackpool whilst pursuing armed criminals.

"To fight for the right, without question or pause."

Printed in Great Britain by Galava Printing Company Limited, Nelson, Lancashire.

Contents

Line drawings in the text are by Roy J. Bancroft. The front cover painting of a representative Lancashire street scene is by Alec Wright, and the back cover study of a Lancashire townscape is from a painting by Harold Hemingway.

Foreword
by Kathleen Eyre

MY HEART belongs to Lancashire and if I had to choose a region in which to spend the whole of my life it would be this dear region of glorious contrasts and astonishing diversity. I love its literature and history. Its variable landscapes never cease to enchant me; its memorials and shrines continually beckon, filling me with wonder; its oddities and landmarks are a perpetual delight, a never-ending source of fascination.

One would have to be very dull indeed to languish here in a state of boredom, for Lancashire, where past and present so breezily commingle, is blessed with charms sufficient for every mood and fancy. There is so much to see and do; so much to read and enjoy; and so many rarities are there to be learned about and discovered. I could long for half a dozen lifetimes to sample all the marvels of this great-hearted county, and for as many more to reflect, and look, and listen. Lancashire, I am quite certain, would never let me down.

This is a county of many faces and multifarious interests, a clattering county, scarred by the great machine age. Great cities and bustling townships go purposefully about their daily business, making and merchandising, trading with the world. It is all there, the grim paraphernalia of industrial activity, the mills and factories, the chimney stacks and canals, the cranes and gantries of dockland, the grime and blackened brick and endless grey roofs sullenly a-glisten. Yet, within easy reach, are areas of supreme quiet and sublime loveliness where city folks and town-dwellers can find solace and refreshment after the week's labours. What happy fortune is theirs, for this is a county of rugged heights, of rolling hills and lonely moorlands; of sparkling rivers tumbling musically through the loveliest of vales; a county of fair green fields and quiet woodlands, or sulking marsh, of little lanes winding through jet-black mossland; a sea-fringed county vibrating with commerce or hushed to stillness in villages, time-honoured; a county where stalls are still set up in the main streets of old market towns and the crowds flock in from all around in cheerful profusion; a county of old grey walls and ruined abbeys, of ancient halls and Tudor farmsteads; of great castles, of soaring spires and grand old churches; of splendid old pubs and tracks as ancient as time.

Within the bounds of old Lancashire the Romans trod, the Angles and Norsemen settled. Celtic missionaries sought their converts, monks laboured, battles were fought and history was made here. The heritage is priceless, and Lancashire is grateful, for this hard-headed, hard-working humorous county, which clings with such pride to its past, also holds with stubborn affection to its legends, its superstitions and its customs.

I love this county of my adoption, I like its mood and temper. And its history, full-blooded and full of savour, is the well-spring of all my joys and satisfactions. The story of Lancashire is a saga of grit and sinew, of saintliness and strife, of inspiration in action, of sturdy endeavour. But the real spirit of Lancashire, the comic genius of the natives, shines out of the literature and folk-speech. "Th' owd Lonkysheer", the language of yesteryear, is on the decline now, its tones and cadences already half-forgotten or consciously erased. Yet our greatest writers employed it unforgettably as a medium for humour and affection, instinctively recognising that a truth, a tenderness, a touch of drollery can often be conveyed in the dialect where it might give offence or fail of effect in standardised English. For that, Lancashire will ever be beholden to her bards, to her poets and songsters, and to her natives who came through the hard times with irrepressible good humour. I like to hope that the true Red Rose man will never be separated from the rich, rough, honest tones of his forefathers, that the dialect will survive, sparkling, crackling and alive with all the old magic; and that the engulfing tide of blood-less B.B.C. English will fall back, spent on the rock of independent Lancashire.

It was my great pleasure, in 1973, to introduce my friend, Bob Dobson, to the ranks of Lancashire writers. His collection of "Lancashire Nicknames and Sayings" added greatly to my know-ledge of the county and has become a constant source of reference, for which I am grateful. It fulfilled a need and proved so popular that the original work, with many additions, comes back to interest, amuse and inform a multitude of new readers. "Moor Poots", "Bolton Trotters", "Chorley Bobs", "Darwen Dud-doos", "Coppull Gawpers"—if you have heard these comical expressions and wondered about them, as I have, here is your opportunity to discover what is known. If you would seek the "Rhubarb City", or "Little Moscow" or even "The War Office" in Lancashire; if you would track down the "Watter-walkers", "Shaft-wratchers", "Cuckoos" or "Pie-cans", this survey, outcome of long patient research and happy wanderings, will cast a beam of cheerful light on your path.

I congratulate Bob Dobson, friend and fellow-member of the Lancashire Authors' Association, and commend his enlightening collection of "Lancashire Nicknames and Sayings" to everyone who would know more about this fascinating county. I am perfectly certain that it will raise a few smiles, settle many arguments, give hours of entertainment, and answer any number of questions.

KATHLEEN EYRE.

"Kate's Pad",
Lime Grove,
LYTHAM ST. ANNES.

Preface

THIS BOOK is a follow-on of its first edition which is now both enlarged and corrected. I want to explain that the nick-names and sayings found in these pages are those which have some connection with townsfolk or townships, and not merely the mouthings of Lancashire folk. Such proverbial phrases are to be found recorded in the pages of our literary heritage. How right was Edward Kirk when he told the Manchester Literary Club: "Folk Sayings are not merely verbal curiosities, but in many cases the condensed wisdom of thoughtful, sensible men who have left their utterances, but not their names, behind."

I must again thank those Lancashire historians, librarians, writers and students who have helped me in my collecting and recording. For their special kindness, I thank Kathleen Eyre and Roy Bancroft for decorating my book, each in their own way. Oh yes, I thank you for reading it. Do please enjoy it.

Staining, Blackpool.
March 1977.

Types of Nicknames

Pigs. It is strange that the pig appears little in the folk lore of Lancashire with the exception of the pig on t'wall and the pig which moved the church foundations, both of which themes are found in several places. Pigs were kept by many families prior to the advent of large factories and provided food for the families. They occur with some frequency in inventories from the 16th century onwards. A pig census was held in 1871 at Ashton-under-Lyne and 524 were counted in the borough at a time when factories were in full swing. Examples:— Stretford (Porkhampton), Rochdale (Bacon Makers), Clitheroe (Bacon Eaters), Tottington (Pig o't'wall).

Work. Industries were, and still are, localised in many ways and for many reasons. Most of these industries grew out of the Industrial Revolution. Lancashire has been called "the first industrial society". In some cases, nicknames were given to people just because they were associated with a particular industry. Examples:— Denton (Hatters), Atherton (Sparrowbills), Warrington (Wires) and Droylesden (Jam Town).

Food. Simple, and thus cheap, foods were the fare of our ancestors, but they liked delicacies as a special treat to tickle the palate. In the first place these delicacies were bought at fairs, though the products of the pig provided basic meals for many. It is strange that the potato does not appear in nicknames. Some delicacies, too, do not appear, such as brandysnaps, arvill cake (eaten at funerals) and simnel cake, though Bury was famed for its simnel cake. (Simnel Sunday became what we know as Mothering Sunday.) For a good selection of the delicacies of the 1860s, read Samuel Laycock's poem "Bowton's Yard". Examples: Bury (Black Puddings), Eccles (Cakers), Ormskirk (Gingerbreads), Waterfoot (Sad Cakers), Green Howarth (Humbug Land), Farnworth (Rhubarb Eaters).

Sport. The early sports of much of Lancashire were hunting, racing, boxing and wrestling. However time was found for sport I do not know. The only name to come from this period was from the all-in wrestling, or purring matches. Later on the masses began to follow football and rugby teams, and it became difficult to know when a nickname referred to a town or a team. Examples:— Pendlebury (Purrers), Burnley (Turfers), Nelson (Seedillers), St. Helens (Saints).

Humour. To attempt to analyse the Lancashire man's humour is a task I cannot undertake. It is far too complex. In it will be found pride, sarcasm, irony, ridicule at least. The idiot is universally scoffed at in a friendly way, and that characteristic of gawmlessness—not peculiarly Lancastrian — comes through in many nicknames. Examples:— Oswaldtwistle (Gobbinland), Shaw (Gawbies), Charnock Richard (Cabbage Heads), Chorley (Petty Door Bangers) and Royton (Wratchers).

"The great majority of place-rhymes are most uncomplimentary to the places to which they refer, a fact which probably accounts for their gradually falling into disuse. Yet their interest is such that it should be worthwhile to rescue them from oblivion and to hand them on to succeeding generations to be treasured as curiosities, rather than to be used as weapons of offence." — Extract from "Place Proverbs and Rhymes, with some sayings and superstitions of Lancashire", by Samuel Whitmore Partington, 1910.

Diminutive. A big word to illustrate that there are several nicknames which liken the subject to some larger, well-known place. These are really a sub-division of the humorous type. As examples, see the **"Little India"** in Preston, the **"Little London"** at Forton, Lancaster, and remember that there must be many a **"Little Blackpool"**.

Accrington Bricks
(see opposite)

Lancashire Nicknames and Sayings

ACCRINGTON

Accrington Shotheads. A shothead is a name for the small fish with the big head better known as the Bullhead or Miller's thumb. It is a sarcastic allusion to the imaginary largeness of the Accringtonian's head, and refers to "big-headedness" in the boastful sense, possibly occasioned by the Accringtonian's intense pride in his town. And I should know—I am one.

Accrington Bricks. Not a nickname at all, but a product for which the town is famous. Two local brick-making works obtained the clay for the bricks from local quarries. To say that a house was built of Accrington brick is to infer quality building.

A township within Accrington's boundaries is Baxenden, known locally only as **"Bash"**.

AINSWORTH, near Bury

Cocky Moorites. Cocky Moor is the part of Ainsworth on both sides of Bury Old Road and west of Starling Road. In practice, except perhaps locally where exactness matters, the whole village is known as Cocky Moor.

Cocky Moor Snakes and **Snakeland.** A traditional poem, "The ballad of Cocky Moor", tells of a man fleeing from the moor in terror after finding what he thinks is a monster snake. It is examined by the rest of the townsfolk, and found to be a lady's feather boa. Outsiders naturally poked fun at the inhabitants after this chap gave the whole village a reputation for dimness. Harland's "Ancient Ballads and Songs of Lancashire" has notes on the poem, which is also contained in the book on the history of the village by the Rev. Bullock, a local minister.

Coccium. This Roman name was for a garrison in Lancashire. The exact site is generally thought to be at Wigan or Horwich, but Ainsworth folk believe that it could well have been at Ainsworth. Note the similarity between Cocky and Coccium. The Roman road from Manchester to Ribchester did pass through the village. It is on a straight line drawn between the two camps. The Radcliffe Local History Society has had aerial photographs taken to investigate the theory.

Ashton Rickers. The name has several possible derivations. Firstly the disease known as rickets was prevalent in Ashton, which at one time was noted for bandy-legged and knock-kneed inhabitants, but the end of malnutrition after the Cotton Famine of the 1860s put an end to the disease. Secondly, to rick means to rattle or scold. I think this has little to do with the nickname. Thirdly, ricking was the sound of clogs making a metallic clang or clatter on stone pavements. This can be compared with the Darwen nickname for the clog sound—"Artillery". The local historian John Cassidy favours this derivation as the most likely.

Fourthly rickers was the name given to two pieces of bone which one held by the fingers and rattled together in a certain way to produce a musical (?) "ricking" noise. This instrument was used as an accompaniment to clog dancing, or as a solo performance. It was an instrument similar to "the magic spoons". **Ash'un Rickers**—a jocular name for the inhabitants of Ashton-under-Lyne—FET*. Taylor also mentions that a rick or ricker is a name for a watchman's rattle. This would be in common use up to the advent of the modern policeman, but rattles were not carried much after the 1850s. There was a newspaper, "The Ashton Ricker" in the 1840s, and a copy exists in the Ashton Library. See also Wright's Dialect Dictionary for "Rickers".

Duck on Muffin. A localised name without apparent meaning, but possibly connected with the eating of such a delicacy on the occasion of fairs.

Ashton Mashers. A masher is the equivalent of a modern "smasher" or dandy. A music hall song known as "The Mashers' Song" was certainly in use at the turn of the century, 1900. It can be compared with "The Burnley Mashers' Song" and is no doubt from the same origin with different local street names added.

In January 1791 a thunderstorm cracked the parish church steeple. By 1818 the church had ten bells. This gave rise to a rhyme, which can be compared with a similar one in Preston and at places in Yorkshire:— "Proud Ashton, poor people—Ten bells in a cracked steeple".

* For references, see page 80.

ASPULL

Moor Poots. Before the Industrial Revolution, Aspull was known as Aspull Moor. The inhabitants were thought to be as immature or simple as a poot, which is Anglo-Saxon for pullet. In the Lancashire dialect, poot is used for pullet and occurs in several nicknames. Even today, a moor-poot is an immature grouse.

ASTLEY BRIDGE, near Bolton

Holy City. This was due to the large number of churches and chapels there at one time, or possibly due to the "superior" attitude of residents towards non-residents.

ATHERTON

Chowbent. I think it best to quote from VCH on the Atherton—Chowbent connection:— The name of Chowbent which is still associated with Atherton has had several variants including Chollebynt and Shollebent in 1350, and the name probably derives from Chowe's Field. The first syllable is almost certainly a proper name and references to a local family called Cholle or Chowe occur in 1535, 1616 and 1725. Contrary to popular belief Chowbent was not synonymous with Atherton but was the name given to a part of the town only, probably the area around the Parish Church.

Bent folk. Obviously a contraction of Chowbent folk. **Chowbent** was famed for gawmlessness, an honour it shared with several other towns. **Chowbent Sparrowbills.** A sparrowbill, now corrupted to read sparable, is a headless nail for soles and heels of boots. Nailmaking was the traditional trade in Atherton, carried on in cottages there until about 1906. The industry was replaced by the making of specialised nuts and bolts.

Sparrowbill dumplings. Sparrowbill nails were sold in pound bags resembling dumplings.

Axon tells of a traditional saying: **"Neither in Cheshire nor Chowbent"** which was an emphatic way of stating the absence of someone or something. Irwin, in LBY, refers to Athertonians as **"Cocky Moorites"**, but this is an obvious mistake, as Cocky Moor is in Ainsworth, near Bury.

Chowbent grubs. Bridge records this saying as meaning those old nails which one meets with when sawing old wood. Today, joiners call nails "Birmingham dove-tails".

AUDENSHAW

Audenshaw Otters. No proper explanation for this nickname can be made except to say that it rolls off the tongue easily. There were several nicknames in various parts of the county which did this, though the majority also had a meaning.

11

BACUP

Bacup Buttercups. The football team did play in yellow jerseys.
Bacup, the place where nettles won't grow. This saying, common
in the Rossendale Valley, is one of derision and nothing to do with
the clay subsoil of the area.

Bacup was called **Giddy Meadows** when Bacup was a small
village in the Forest of Rossendale. A **"Bacup look"** is an
examination with the fingers.

BAMBER BRIDGE

T' brig. Locals still contract the township's proper name to this
one. EDD records that brig means bridge, but the locals need no
telling of this though they may be surprised to learn that the
word is used in Scottish and Midland counties' dialects, as well
as in Northern England. Locals were once called **"briggers"** and
possibly **"brig enders"**, though a prominent local historian,
George Birtill, has not encountered the names.

BAMFORD, near Rochdale

T' War Office—a jocular name for the village of Bamford—FET.
By coincidence rather than by design, I suspect, a pub bearing
the name of that great man at the war office of this nation—
Sir Winston Churchill—was opened in Bamford in the early 1970s.

BARROWFORD

"Like Barrowford, all on one side". Carr suggests that this local
saying has arisen from the fact that the village was built almost
entirely on one side of the river, known as Pendle Water. A local
man, the Rev. Hartley, composed a song, to be sung to the tune
"Bonny Colne", called "Barrowford all on one side".
T' Gaumless. This was the name given to a well in Barrowford.
Blakey doesn't tell us why, but he does tell a nice tale about a
little girl whose granny lived near it. She was asked one day
which granny she had been to visit, and replied, "My gaumless
grandmother". The original well, a drinking trough, was opened
in 1847, and replaced by a newer fountain in 1911. A local poet
wrote a humorous rhyme to the praise of "Gaumless Water".

BESWICK, part of Manchester

Bessick—FET. The "w" is omitted from many words in dialect.

BILLINGE, near Wigan

Billinge Chairs. Chair-making was carried on there in the 18th and early 19th centuries. On the 1849 O.S. map, "Chair Wood" is marked near Longshaw Common. The wood for the chairs is supposed to have come from Chair Wood. Quarrying and check weaving were other local industries at this time. The Wood was dug up a few years ago for opencast coal mining and replanted by the Bankes family of Winstanley Hall a little further to the South.

BLACKBURN

Blegburn—the dialect pronunciation. **Blegburn dud-doos.** This name arises from the habit of the Blackburnians of saying "dud do" instead of "did do".
Blegburn Billies. EDD gives several column inches to "Billy". The word seems to have two main meanings—a brother and a simpleton, though it can mean "friend", "lover" or "bull". A "billy" was a contraction for the hat known as a "billycock". I can find no reference to suggest that either of the main meanings is the most likely one in this case. A similar name exists for Bolton men.
Good husband teawn. Teddy Ashton mentions this in his poem "Tum Fowt Christmas" in the Teddy Ashton Annual for 1905. I have not encountered a reason for the name, but think that he believed Blackburn to be so, and probably coined the name himself, as he did with others. He wrote a poem "A lass fro' Chorley" as if it were "good wife town". I have heard of an old lady, recently passed away, who, when one gave her a cup of tea that she relished for its weakness and sweetness, said after tasting it: "Oh, that's good husband tea". She was a Blackburn lady, and her husband was a Darrener.

The writer Richard Dugdale described Blackburn as **"that abode of poetry and politics, piety and picking-sticks".**

BLACKLEY, Manchester

Blackley Lions. Derived no doubt from the number of inns there named after the king of beasts. FET:— A jocular term for the inhabitants of Blackley. Blackley is pronounced "Blakeley".
Crab Village is the oldest part of Higher Blackley. The derivation is probably from the crab-apple trees which at one time would grow there.

BLACKPOOL

"Sand grown uns" are Blackpool-born people. The name is to be found in a slightly varied form, however, to mean people born on the West Lancashire coast from Liverpool to Morecambe. The name certainly means anyone born on the Fylde coast. See Kathleen Eyre's book—"Sand Grown".

Blackpool Skenners. Langford Saunders, a Blackpool resident, wrote in "Lancashire Humour and Pathos" (p. 87):— "With the sun so bright, they couldn't stand the brilliance. They passed it on by looking at others. So, when you see anybody wi' a breawn face an' neck an' a gradely squint in their e'en, be sure they, or their forebears, were born in Blackpool". I have not encountered this name elsewhere.

"Death is a stranger to Blackpool". A clergyman named Thornber, writing in 1837, said that the inhabitants of Blackpool had always been remarkable for their longevity, and mentioned this saying. Undoubtedly it is a healthy place due to the sea breezes. Dickens visited the place and spoke well of the quality of the air. See Kathleen Eyre's—"Fylde Folk: Moss or Sand", and "Seven Golden Miles".

Blackpudlians. Blackpool people are now referred to by this name. Blackpoolians would be the more proper name, and perhaps the name now used is a reference to the Black Puddle (instead of Pool) from which the town gets its name. I suggest that it is because it contains that essence of wit which characterises so many of the nicknames.

Writing in a Blackpool holiday guide issued by the Corporation early in the century, Harold L. Whiteside styles Blackpool as **"The City of Health and Pleasure".** Another popular writer styled it **"Th' Weighvers' Paradise"** for reasons that anyone familiar with the history of Lancashire mill towns knows well.

Blackpolitans. A name similar to Blackpudlians, this term was used in a Blackpool newspaper in 1876. It sounds a shade finer than Blackpudlians.

Little Blackpool. In Lancashire there must be several places which have been given this name. For instance, in Accrington, the name was given to a few places all of which were play-places for children, all having those magic ingredients found in the real Blackpool—water (stream, not sea), sand (often imaginary) and of course, perpetual sunshine. It is a name which conjures up happy memories.

Writing in a holiday brochure, G. R. Sims called Blackpool **"A Wonderland by the Sea",** and continuing this theme, present-day publicists call the famed Blackpool Illuminations **"The greatest free show on earth".**

BOLTON

Bolton—Bowton in the dialect. **Bowton Billies.** See FET and the notes on "billy" in Blackburn.

Bowton Trotters. The best authorities discount the connection between this nickname and the succulent dish known as "trotters" which are really sheep's feet (by means of which sheep "trot"). This dish has always been popular in the Bolton area, as many as 60,000 being sold in one week at a time when they were most popular. So what is the reason for the nickname? An old meaning of "to trot" was "to banter, hoax, tease, make fun of". Bamford, writing in 1854, defined the verb as "to joke, satirize, provoke, mislead by way of amusement to the trotter". We might call it leg-pulling.

There are accounts of trotting incidents in Whittle, Bolton-le-Moors, in 1855 and a famous incident involved one Squire Kay in Richardson's "Reminiscences of 40 Years in Bolton", 1880. A painting depicting a trotting incident is to be seen in the Hall i' th' Wood Museum, Bolton. It shows two men, each standing with one leg in a pail of boiling water. They are doing so for a bet. One is obviously in great pain, the other pain-free. The reason for that is that the latter, the trotter, has a cork leg. The onlookers think it a great joke.

Langford Saunders, in his "Lancashire Humour and Pathos" (p. 86) put forward another possible explanation of the trotting nickname. He says that at one time "children came thick and fast, there was no work, and men had to walk fast, or trot, to Manchester, and that was 24 miles both roads."

The Bolton Wanderers Football Club, has had the nickname "Trotters" applied to its team. This has no doubt popularised the name, which is probably the best known of the Lancashire nicknames.

Bowton Chaps. See the saying about gentlemen, men, chaps and fellas in Liverpool.

Steam Engine Land. This name was coined by the Lancashire writer Charles Allen Clarke (Teddy Ashton), 1863-1935, writing about the area around his native Bolton which was at one time known as Bolton-le-Moors. It contrasts with the name he coined for the Fylde — Windmill Land. See his book "Moorlands and Memories".

"Geneva of the North". The brand of Christianity known as Calvinism had many followers in Bolton, and so the town gained a reputation for the prevalence of the doctrines of John Calvin, a resident of Geneva.

The Bolton humourist J. T. Staton applied several nicknames to the inhabitants of Bolton. At various times he used the following, all having some connection with eating:— **Porritch Eiters, Jannock Chaumpers, Fried Prato Munchers, Berm and Meight Dumplin Devourers.** I suspect they were names of his own invention.

Allen Clarke had the wit to try to cash in on the locals' pride in their Trotters nickname by giving the name to a newspaper he published 1891-93.

BOOTLE

"Go to Bootle". An expression which is a half-profanity intended by the deliverer to give the message to the recipient that he should go to that place where the devil lives.

Bootle Buckoes. The Merseyside sage Frank Shaw revealed to the world in a wonderful series of articles in the Lancashire Dialect Society Journal (1958-60) that some local words had meanings which were different to the commonly accepted ones. Such a word is buckoe (also buck, or rowdie) which simply means an inhabitant of the criminal underground. I had always thought that a buckoe was a tough fighting man, but Shaw states that this is not necessarily so. It is noteworthy that the term does not crop up elsewhere in Lancashire.

The town has a reputation for toughness, as shown in the phrase **"Bootle, where the bugs fly backwards and the barmaids eat their young".** That sounds to me a phrase of recent Merseyside invention.

BRETHERTON, near Chorley

In a marvellous little book compiled a few years ago by the members of the Women's Institutes of Lancashire, the wives of Bretherton told the world that in former years the folk up the road at Hoole called Bretherton **"Th' edge o' leet"**. It reminds me of an old Lancashire description of nightfall—Th' edge o' dark. The Stalybridge poet Sam Hill wrote a beautiful poem with that title. It concerns a man passing into another world from this. Edwin Waugh described the time:—

> As the day-end faded into night,
> An' th' twileet's shadows deepened reawnd.

BRINDLE, near Chorley

Brindle Cuckoos. It was said of Brindle folk that, wishing to keep summer, they built a wall round the cuckoos, which flew away "and another row of stones would have done it". It refers to their simplicity. The name is to be found elsewhere in the country. See Chipping.

BURNLEY

Burnley Mashers. The expression means "smashers" or dandies. There was an old music hall song, "The Two Burnley Mashers" popular in Burnley early in the century. The words and music are available in Burnley Public Library. The song is probably a parody on "Jolly Fine Company" which was in a printed song book published by McGlennon's before World War 1. There was a dance to the song. See Lancashire Evening Telegraph 3.10.1958 and Lancashire Authors' Association "Record" No. 223.

In his poem "The Masher O", the Halifax poet J. C. Trott, writing in the latter end of last century, described the masher as a person of little virtue, a wastrel in fancy clothes. One verse goes:—

> The idle, worthless Masher O
> The blase, rakish Masher O
> T'was Nature who produced the man,
> But "brass" produced the Masher O.

Burnley Haymakers. This is not a nickname, but the title of a song written by Mr. Cottam of Hurst Green—see ABSL. **Burnley Turfers.** The Burnley footfall club ground is called Turf Moor and this nickname for all Burnley folk has almost certainly arisen from this football connection. The club historian, the Rev. David Wiseman, suggests that the name would arise in the period 1890 to 1914.

Burnley Bobs. In the Teddy Ashton Lancashire Annual for 1925, Allen Clarke (Teddy Ashton) specifically states that he has not heard of any nickname for Burnley folk, and goes on to suggest that we could call them **Burnley Loomers** because of their weaving connection or Burnley Bobs because they spend their money lavishly when on holiday. This is proof that he invented town nicknames. I can trace no other use of these particular nicknames.

Burnley Watter-Walkers. It had been suggested to me, when preparing notes for the first edition, that it was a legend, without support, that at some time in the past the folk of Burnley had been invited to watch a Padiham man walk across the river Calder without getting his feet wet, and that, gawmless-like, they had turned up believing it was possible. I now have evidence that this event actually took place in 1854. I have discovered the existence of a poster which reads:—

Padiham Wakes
Unparalleled Feet

"Mons. Signor Professor De La Unsinque, from the Villa Aquatorius, has the distinguished honour to announce to the Admirers of the Wonderful that he will repeat his aquatorial experiment as performed at the Royal Baths of Gottenburg of WALKING ON THE WATER on Monday next, on the River Calder, at Padiham. The water to be taken a little above the bridge at four o'clock P.M. Professor De La Unsinque's valet will attend to receive the offerings of the visitors. M.S.P. De La Unsinque is Web-Footed. The Professor will afterwards take a drive on the river in his quatic equipage—N.B. The geese will previously parade the banks of the river."

We don't have practical jokers like that nowadays, and though it has been said that the name Watter-Walkers has been given to Padiham folk, the name seems to have been more commonly applied to **Burnleyites.** In her article in "Lancashire Life" a few years ago, Jessie Birtwistle reveals the identity of the hoaxers, one of them being John Birtwistle, landlord of the Bridge Inn, near to which the geese lined the banks. No doubt they bought ale from him. See also the "Burnley Gazette" of 25th March, 1893.

"T' Gawmless." The sarcastic wit of Burnley folk was, many years ago, turned upon a gas lamp standard, giving a light which was "owt but bright" and which stood for many years in the centre of Burnley, at the junction of Manchester Road with St. James Street. It was later replaced by an electric tram standard, but the name remained in use. It was a meeting place for men intent on building the Empire and setting the world to right by day, and for courting couples by night.

Burnley Dud-doos. The Lancashire writer Ben Brierley ("Ab-o'-th-Yate") uses this name in a story about some people he met at Blackpool, probably about 1890. I suspect that he has mistaken the folk from Burnley with those from Blackburn, as the name is most commonly associated with Blackburn, and his connection of Burnley with "dud-doos" is the only one I have come across. **Burnleyites** is the collective noun for inhabitants of the town. In past times a Burnley-bred person was called a **"Shumpty"** and a non-native a **"Switchemer"**.

BURY

Bury Muffs. A jocular term for the inhabitants of Bury—FET. The origin is not certain but one suggestion is that it originated from the times when cockfighting was popular, and the crest of a hen was called a muff. Later the term was applied to Bury Football Club when they lost a match. To "marry muff" in dialect slang means "nonsense" and thus the name could be an allusion to the leg-pulling humour of Buryites. John Hartley's Clock Almanack of 1869 refers to "muff" as meaning to make little noise—"He never muffed".

Bury Puddings. Another jocular term—FET. Black puddings, for which the town is famous, have been made there since at least 1818 on a commercial basis. The ingredients include pig's blood, spices, fat and skins from animal intestines. The pig figured largely in the diet of the Lancastrian before the Industrial Revolution, and since that time, too.

Bury Muffins. Probably derived from "muffs" but possibly connected with "rag-a-muffins" who after all are mischievous imps. The town is not famous for its muffins—bread cakes. **Bury Shakers.** In the final of the Lancashire Senior Cup in 1892 the term "shakers" arose. Starting as only second favourites, Bury scored twice to win the game. During the game, a Bury official excitedly shouted out: "We'll give 'em a shaking. In fact, we're the shakers". The phrase became a nickname in common use and referred to the townsfolk generally.

Bury Bulldogs. No origin is known, but I suggest that it rolls easily off the tongue and is a reference to the tenacity of Bury people.

Bury Sweeps. The name preserves an ancient libel on the strange appearance presented by the earliest Bury Militia or Fencibles at their first muster or parade. The men probably looked as smart as chimney sweeps.

Black puddings—sausages made from pig's blood, pork fat and groats (1901) FET. See "Bury Puddings" above. **Dicky Bird Estate.** There is a council house estate in Bury on which the streets are named after birds, and in consequence the name "dicky bird" has been applied. It compares with the "Blue City" estate in Prescot. Besides being famed for the quality of black puddings, the town was in past days famed too for simnel cake.

CARNFORTH

"Steamtown". In the days of "real" trains, Carnforth was a main centre, with sheds housing row upon row of iron giants, and many of the townsfolk were railwaymen. With the decline of the system, the town lost its importance, but there was born an idea that we ought to preserve the nostalgia of the days of steam. A museum was opened at Carnforth in 1969 which is aimed at showing the public the glories of steam locomotives. The organisers used the splendid name "Steamtown" for their project. I can find no evidence that the name was in use before that time, though it could well have been given to the whole town.

CHADDERTON

I have traced no nickname for the town or the townsfolk, but a name exists for the residents of a particular road—Foxdenton Road, Chadderton. They are known as **Foxyites.** This is a little unusual because normally residents of a particular road or lane are called—Laners, as in Denton Laners for the residents of Denton Lane, Chadderton. In such cases I have omitted reference to the names.

CHARNOCK RICHARD, near Chorley

Charnock Richard Cabbage Heads. Very simply a term of derision.

CHILDWALL, South Liverpool

In a rhyme—See Prescot and Huyton—Childwall is referred to as **Childow.** It seems that Childwall's parish church was noted for its bells and its singers, and the townsfolk for working hard and playing hard.

CHIPPING

Chipping Cuckoos. Wishing to keep summer, the inhabitants built a wall round the cuckoos which unfortunately flew away ... "but another row of stones would have done it". From this saying we can infer that Chipping folk were simple minded. See Brindle. **It cuckoos in winter out (at) Chipping.** A saying having some reference to the above.

CHORLEY

Chorley Cakes or Cakers. This famous sweet, similar to an Eccles cake, would probably become locally famed before the recipe became more widely known. It may well have been eaten at local fairs, in the same way as were Eccles cakes. There is no baker in the town noted for baking them, but large bakery combines sell to local retailers. The nickname arises from the local delicacy just as others did—see Eccles, Ormskirk.

Chorley Bob. This nickname has two connections. Firstly, a Chorley fire engine was so named in honour of Field Marshal Lord Roberts. The engine was used in the celebrations for Mafeking Night. Bob of course is a contraction for Robert. Secondly, a local passenger train was called "Chorley Bob". It was in a collision in which the driver was fatally injured on 23rd January, 1909.

Chorley Magpies. The name arose from the colours of the town football team, and developed from the nickname of the team to become the nickname for a Chorley person in much the same way as the Turfer from Burnley. **Chorley Corrs or curs.** I can suggest no reason for this nickname. I think it unlikely that the "cur" means "a dog". Urwin, in LBY, suggests that "Bobs", "Corrs" and "Magpies" are all connected with the football team.

Chorley Petty-door bangers. This is probably the most lewd of the nicknames applied to Lancastrians. It suggests some mystique connected with the toilet, and I think is nothing to do with the means of communication referred to in Littlemoss, or Clifton. It is a term of derision which was certainly in use in the 1930s, and almost certainly in use in places other than Chorley. A similar name for some Rossendale Valley township is thought to be in fairly recent usage.

Chorley Mallet-heads. Tradition tells of all Chorley children folk. It is said that when a Clifton villager saw a stranger in the

Clifton Gawpers. This arose from the alleged peculiarity of the receiving a bump on the head from a mallet at birth, "an' that's why they're a bit thick", as an old lady told me.

Chorley Currans. Allen Clarke, writing as Teddy Ashton in Teddy Ashton's "Lancashire Annual" for 1925, records this nickname that he had heard. He suggests that the name may allude to the townsfolk's sweetness or dryness, but I suggest the only reason for the name is the reference it contains to the well-known Chorley cakes, which of course contain currants. Allen Clarke had a wonderful imagination and coined several nicknames.

CLAYTON, Manchester

I have traced no nickname, but a former resident recalls a rhyme which cannot be properly remembered, about the chiming of church bells in Clayton. Research has so far failed to identify the rhyme. Steeples and bells figure frequently in local lore.

CLAYTON GREEN, near Chorley

Clayton Green Wild Ducks. There is a lake or lodge near, frequented by wild fowl.—LBY. The name would probably be a localised one based on fact.

CLIFTON

Rhubarb (or rhuburb in dialect) **town.** Folk from the Manchester conurbation who took wagonette trips would pass through Clifton and see fields of rhubarb plants. They believed that the locals lived off the stuff. See Farnworth, also Galgate for a slight variation on the theme.

street outside he banged his cupboard door. This was a signal to the next-door neighbours to go to see or "gawp at" him. See Littlemoss for a slight variation on this "jungle telegraph" theme.

CLITHEROE

Low Moor Bacon Eaters. Low Moor is now part of this royal and ancient borough. The pig-keeping and bacon-eating tradition of the locals is illustrated by a phrase from a Clitheroe man:—
"In them days, everyone o' them Low Moorites had a pig-sty backside o' his house ... they welly (well nigh—almost) lived on nowt else but bacon from year's end to year's end."—LBY.

Castleites. A nickname coined by a local sports columnist writing of the town cricket team. Still in use, but mainly in the same context.

Clitheroe Caterpillars. This is derived from a plague of caterpillars which invaded Pendle Hill in June 1811, wreaking havoc on the crops. They were finally destroyed by a very severe thunderstorm. A Clitheroe man, Mr. W. Hanson, has written a poem about the event. Irwin, in LBY gives a different story of the plague and a different date—1892. His caterpillars died because they could not eat heather after devouring meadow grass. I favour the former version, based on recorded evidence.

Clitheroe—famous for the three "L's". They are, firstly, **Lime**. The town stands on limestone. A major industry there is concerned with quarrying and cement making. The castle is built of limestone. Lime burning has been carried on for centuries there. Secondly, **Law.** Clitheroe Lords had a reputation in medieval times for strictly enforcing the laws concerning the poor. Clitheroe Castle was the administrative and judicial centre of the Blackburn Hundred. Thirdly, **Latin.** The Clitheroe Royal Grammar School is founded upon an ancient Royal charter, and was originally a seminary. Teaching emphasis for many years lay on Latin, all other subjects being considered secondary.

Pendle Hill is strongly linked with Clitheroe in history, lore and indeed reality. It appears in many of the local sayings recorded by Weeks. Some of them are:—

"As old as Pendle Hill"—in use as early as 1662, and inferring that the subject under discussion is not a new one.

**"When Pendle wears its woolly cap,
Farmers all may take a nap."**

**"When Pendle Hill doth wear a hood,
Be sure, the day will not be good."**

**"If you can't see Pendle, it's raining.
If you can see Pendle, it's going to rain."**

Pendle gets a mention too in other rhymes linking it with Ingleborough and Penyghent.

Clitheroe card players of former days, when deciding to play cards for stakes other than money, would say **"We'll play for the Castle"**, implying that the game was "for love".

The English Appenines was how, with slight variations, the English historians and travellers Camden, Leland and Thoresby described the Pendle Hill countryside. The Lancashire writer Edwin Waugh once wrote of someone that she was **"as fause as one o' th' Pendle Witches"**.

COLNE

Bonny Colne upo' th' hill. This is one of the very few phrases of endearment and praise to be found amongst the many which ridicule towns and townsfolk. See "Bonnie Colne", a poem by a local author and choirmaster, Frank Slater, written in 1873.

The townsfolk are very proud of Colne's dignity and the reference to it in the Domesday Book. In this respect, and in respect of the term of praise referred to above, the town can be compared with Lancaster.

A rhyme adapted to local conditions is:—

> *When Pendle Hill puts on his hat*
> *Ye men of Colne, beware of that:*
> *When Pendle Hill doth clear appear*
> *Ye men of Colne have nought to fear.*

The rhyme has been similarly adapted to many areas in England.

"Like Colne Clock, always at one". Carr tells us that "formerly (pre 1878) a steady person was said to be 'like Colne clock, always at one'", as the clock more often stood than went.

Colne Irons. In the days when clog irons were locally made, any which were extra thick gained this name. I think it unlikely that all irons made in Colne were very thick, as this would be less economical for the town's cloggers, who would be as canny as their colleagues in other towns. Probably the name came to mean those irons specially made in thicker gauge metal.

COPPULL, near Chorley

Coppull Gawpers. To "gawp" is to stare as would an idiot. It must be related to "gawby" or "gaby", which means a simpleton. It is probably a term of derision equivalent to that applied to the folk of neighbouring Charnock Richard—cabbage heads.

COPSTER GREEN, near Whalley

Goose Muck Green. This name arose many years ago, when the villagers, having grazing rights, used to keep geese on the common land in the village. What a grand sight it must have been on Good Fridays when the people from Blackburn and elsewhere walked in parties to Copster Green. Many of the villagers used to put out tables to serve teas to the visitors, and swings were erected on the village green. I suppose their only worry was dodging the goose muck. In Whalley Church is a carving dated 1434 of a man shoeing a goose. This appears to have no connection with Copster Green, but illustrates a proverb. Some similar carvings are to be found in Beverley Minster.

CRAWSHAWBOOTH, Rossendale

Krayshi. This is a dialect contraction of the town name. **Krayshi Ponkers.** Again in the dialect, a ponk is a form of bonk, which means bank or steep hill. Crawshawbooth is surrounded by steep hills. See Tyldesley.

DARCY LEVER, near Bolton

Dolly Tub City. This name probably arose from the number of women who "took in weshin" in the area. The name has no equivalent elsewhere in Lancashire. It probably dates from the middle of the last century, at least. It brings back memories of the dolly tub, scrubbing board, and posser, and social conditions poorer by far than we now know. Incidentally, it occurs to me to record the fact that dolly tubs needed a "dolly" to help get the clothes clean, and this was the wooden device with a cross-piece handle and a three- or four-pronged bottom end which, when swished among the water and clothes, gave what salesmen now call "rotary action". A posser had a straight handle with a copper, conical bottom end.

Aigburth, Liverpool, had a street called Dolly Tub Row, where washing was to be seen hanging across the street on each day of the week except Sunday.

The Dolly Tub (see page 25)

DARWEN

Darren, the dialect pronunciation. **Darren Artillery.** Derived from the sound made by clog irons and soles on flagstones whilst the wearers were hurrying to the mill in a morning. Clogs themselves were known as artillery, simply because men fought with them—and women too on occasions. This was in the "sport" of puncin' or kicking.—See Pendlebury and Wigan.

Darren Steamers. This is a nickname that I cannot properly give a reason for. It is thought to have some connection with the Darwen steam trams. These ran in Darwen between 1881 and 1900. See Rush, "The tramways of Accrington 1886-1932" (1961).

Darren dud-doos. Darwen and Blackburn share a common boundary, and the nickname most commonly applied to Blackburnians is probably equally applicable to Darwenians, who may have shared the habit of saying "du do" instead of "did do".

Darren Salmon. Almost certainly a term carrying with it a certain amount of true Lancashire sarcasm, as it has not been possible for a salmon to live in the River Darwen since the Industrial Revolution due to what we now know as pollution, formerly known as "muck".

Darren Salmon—a jocular term for the inhabitants of Darwen—FET. A "silly story" concerning Darren salmon is recorded in Teddy Ashton's Lancashire Annual for 1925. A local chap was promised the dish by his wife, but on returning home for tea found a red herring on his plate, being assured by his wife that it was "Darren salmon"—the one and the same.

Darren Rawngers (i.e. Rangers). Almost certainly derived from a football team, and probably mis-applied to the townsfolk in much the same way as names for Burnley and Chorley.

Some wit (thought by some to be Robbie Burns), in years gone by composed this rhyme:—

> *Among the hills so bleak and barren*
> *Lies mucky, rotten, little Darren.*

Darren not on the map. It is said that a deputation went from Darwen to interview Lord Russell in order to urge its claims to be created a Parliamentary borough. To their astonishment, he had never heard of Darwen, and on calling for a map of England, found that it wasn't even shown thereon.

DEAN, Rossendale

Deyne Layrocks. The dialect term which means the larks of Dean. Not a nickname, but certainly a name applied to a section of the community in the Dean Valley, Rossendale. The inhabitants there have long been noted for their excellence as musicians, both vocal and instrumental, and it is from this accomplishment that the name Dean Layrocks has arisen. It has certainly been in use for 200 years. See Newbigging, "Lancashire Humour" and Collins, "Rochdale Roundabout", 1960. Rawtenstall Public Library keeps local records of musical interest. A history has been written of the Rossendale Male Voice Choir, surely a descendant of the Dean Layrocks. Dean means "shut-in gill".

DENTON

Denton Padding Cans. A "can" was a term used in the hatting trade, to describe a large sateen bag used by out-door (i.e. at home) workers for carrying hats for trimming. The bag sometimes contained a wood and wire stand to hold the hats. A group of hats, say 12, was known as a "pad". The word "padding" in this sense, though, is with the meaning of "leg-pulling, mischievously" —see the Bolton term "trotting". This information came from an elderly resident of Denton who was connected with the hatting trade.

Denton Mad Hatters. Again the derivation is from the hatting trade for which Denton has long been famous, and the term was found in a book of 1899. Lewis Carroll first wrote of his Mad Hatter in 1865, so the name probably arose some time between the two dates. **Denton—Hatters or Hatters' Town.** The inhabitants were known as **"the Hatters"**, from the hatting industry carried on there since as early as the 17th century. This is one of the few towns to have a nickname applied to it which is derived from the trade of the town. See Middleton, "Annals of Hyde 1899".

DOLPHINHOLME, near Lancaster

Pewwy. As a contrast to "Wewwy" (the neighbouring village of Over Wyresdale). A purely localised name used by boys of the area up to the 1930s.

DOWNHAM

There can be few people who can think of Downham as anything but **"The prettiest village in Lancashire"**, since it first achieved success in the annual competitions to find Lancashire's best-kept village. **Downham Diamonds** or **Downham Stones.** McKay mentions crystals found in the vicinity of Downham, said to be equal in lustre to real gems. Later writers tell of them being brilliant, hard stones of a semi-precious nature.

Rising above Downham is the hill described by local poet Henry Holding as **"Pendle, a hoary hill of evil fame".**

DROYLSDEN

Droylsden Foomerts (or foomuts or foomarts)—FET. A foomart (O.E.D. and Wright) is (a) a polecat, (b) a term of offensive contempt for a person or thing, (c) a sharp, quick-witted person or (d) a simpleton. The popular meaning seems to be (a), though for what reason I do not know. If comparison were to be made with other towns, then any of the alternatives would suffice. See FET —Foomert dog, a dog for hunting foomerts.

Droylsden — Silly Country, and Droylsden people — **Sillyites.** The origin of these names is not known, but they are obviously derisory and sarcastic. **Droylsden—Jam Town.** Robertson's jam works is in the town. It was started there in the last quarter of the last century.

"More fools pass through Droylsden than live in it." This saying, common throughout the country, has simply been adapted to local conditions. **Droylsden, where they put pig o't' wall.** This story illustrating simplicity of local people is repeated at several places in the county, and indeed in the country. See Tottington. **World's End.** For well over a hundred years, that part of the town near the Littlemoss boundary has had this name. One historian suggested that it originated as "Weald's end", or the end of the weald (a moor), but the present name is quite appropriate when one considers the road petering out into the wilderness of Ashton Moss. There is a World's End Farm in the area, thus illustrating how a nickname can grow into common and proper usage.

ECCLES

Eccles Cakeites. The origin of Eccles cakes is of religious significance, as is simnel cake. It was originally sold at fairs or wakes. In "Eccles—the growth of a Lancashire town", Johnston suggests that the cakes were made in the 17th century, but the earliest authentic reference is 1796 when James Birch made them. In 1810 he moved from his shop near the parish church to one across the street. His business passed from him to his nephew, then to his grandson. Meanwhile William Bradburn, a former employee of Birch, started up business as cake-maker and grocer in Birch's old shop. Some rivalry started. Other local shops sold the cakes, and they were exported as early as 1818. In 1880, three million Eccles cakes a year were sold. The nickname is no longer in use.

Liverpudlians, with their characteristic wit, have been known to call Eccles cakes "fly cemeteries" which they pronounce "symettries". Surely I needn't explain why.

As thrunk as Eccles Wakes, no room areawt. Thrunk means crowded (the word is "thrang" or "throng" in other parts of the county), so this phrase means "As crowded as Eccles Wakes, no room out of doors." Joseph Bridge recorded this saying and a similar one referring to Cheadle, Cheshire.

"Do they Eccles as like" and **"Go to Eccles".** In both these, you must substitute the word "Hell" for Eccles to obtain the meaning. They were probably used when the speaker did not want to offend or show himself up in his company. There is a similar expression used in Bootle. F. E. Taylor calls it "an evasive expletive". The dialect writer Ben Brierley used the former expression.

EDGWORTH, near Bolton

Edgworth—Bogland. This arises from the peaty nature of the land there. It is almost unique in the form of derivation.

EVERTON

Everton Toffeemen. A name now applied to the Everton F.C. was formerly applied to the townsfolk. Everton toffee was made by Molly Bushell (1736-1813) in Everton township, which is now in the city of Liverpool. Molly Bushell has been adopted as the mascot of Everton F.C. Supporters' Club and is shown on their lapel badge. Everton toffee is an example of a local food becoming applied as a nickname.

In early 1973, the condition of three blocks of flats in the area had become so bad through the work of vandals that locals named them **"The Piggeries"**.

FAILSWORTH

Failsworth Polecats (Powcats in dialect). The nickname may be purely derisory, as in that applied to Droylsden, or it may be a combination of wit and derision. The wit would be that it contains reference to the famous Failsworth Pole, a celebrated point in the centre of the town. There has been a Failsworth Pole in the town, not in the same spot, since 1746. It was formerly the centre of local life.

Failsworth Foomerts. A foomert is (amongst other meanings) a polecat, or a simpleton. See Droylsden. **Failsworth Gawbies.** This nickname is the most common of the terms of derision. A gaby or gawby is a stupid person or simpleton.

Failsworth—Dark Town. This name arose from the defective street lighting there. I have been unable to "date" the name with any degree of accuracy, though it would probably be born in the late years of the last century and the early years of this one, when gas street lighting was becoming common to all industrial townships.

A rhyme which has been adapted to several places throughout the country has some historical connection based on an unfinished church in the 1840s at Failsworth:

> *Failsworth township, a queer people.*
> *An Irish parson and a church 'bout steeple.*

The famed Lancashire writer and poet Ben Brierley, known too by his pen name of Ab'o'th'Yate (which means Ab of the Gate) was born at Failsworth and a plaque is displayed on the house he lived in. Ben heard that the Failsworth Pole was to be taken down and he wrote a "Lament for the Failsworth Pole" as if it were the Pole lamenting. Ben's brother bard, Samuel Laycock, wrote these lines about Failsworth:— "For while London reared Dickens and others as great, It was Failsworth that reared the renowned Ab'o'th'Yate."

FARNWORTH

Farnworth Rhubarb Eaters. This nickname was given by the people from the far side of Manchester who saw the fields of growing rhubarb, which they probably pronounced "Rhuburb", when they made trips by wagonette to or through the area around Farnworth. For similar nicknames, see Clifton, Walkden and Galgate.

Farnworth Freaks. A jocular term applied to the inhabitants of Farnworth—FET. A large mental hospital and work-house, the Fishpool Institute, was opened on the Farnworth-Bolton boundary in 1861. It would then be far from the Farnworth built-up area, but would no doubt be associated with the town in the minds of others. The inhabitants, particularly the mental patients, would be thought "freakish" and thus the name arose. One reason for the nickname sticking for some years—it is not now in use—is the easy way in which the phrase rolls off the tongue. The Institute served the greater Bolton area.

Halshaw Moor. This is not a nickname, but a name often applied to Farnworth. It is wrongly applied to the town as a whole, but in fact was only a part of the town. The area which now comprises most of the shopping centre was Halshaw Moor. It is a contraction of "Alec Shaw's Moor", a piece of common ground. At one time the local railway station was known as "Farnworth and Halshaw Moor". See Barton, "History of Farnworth and Kearsley".

FLEETWOOD

Fleetwood arose from sandhills and rabbit warrens in the 1840s, and is thus Lancashire's first "new town", but it does not have any town nickname. However, a street there, Abercrombie Road, was at one time considered a "posh" street and was locally nicknamed **"Skippers Row"** because of the number of fishing-boat skippers who lived there. As times have changed other roads have become fashionable. The consideration of some streets as "posh" has long gone on. Samuel Laycock, the Lancashire poet, wrote "Quality Row" about a Stalybridge Street. On the Fleetwood boundary near the I.C.I. works is Springfield Terrace, a small terrace of cottages. The townsfolk still call the area **"Burglars' Alley"**. One train of thought is that the name arose because of the exposed situation and the proximity of the houses to Blackpool—where there were burglars.

Dodwell records a local saying:—

"The chill waste of Lapland could only compare
With wild Rossall Warren, unsheltered and bare."

Rossall is part of Fleetwood, at its boundary with Cleveleys, and the word warren illustrates what I said in the first line.

It amazes me that there is no nickname or saying which places on record Fleetwood's association with the fishing industry.

FORMBY

Formby Cockles. The men of Formby would be sea-going fishermen who would no doubt take cockles to help gain a livelihood, and the cockles would be relished as a delicacy before the days when the cockle beds became polluted by industrial waste. Thus the name has both food and work connections.

Formby had, perhaps still has, a reputation for poshness. A person enjoying quick promotion might be said by a Scouse to "be livven in Formby nex' ".

Poverty Walk. An article in a 1972 "Lancashire Life" magazine by a Formby resident told us that, when he was a boy, the path now named Montague Road was known as Poverty Walk. I suppose it could have been a poor area, but in view of Formby's reputation, and as the houses there now are far from impoverished, I feel that the Merseyside wits have been at it again. See Edith Kelly's book "Viking Village, the story of Formby" (1973).

FORTON

The M6 motorway (Britain's first, don't forget) was built through tranquil Forton in the early 1960s. The service area that was built there had a tower that brought the future to the present, and when seen from the hills and fields nearby, particularly at night, the whole place reminded locals of the great metropolis, and so they named it **"Little London"**.

FRECKLETON, near Kirkham

Yockleton. There is little doubt that this name is derived from **"Yokel Town"**. Freckleton is set among large, flat fields, many of them Ribble-washed. It was a sleepy, country village before the coming of high-speed traffic and housing estates, and we all know that such villages are peopled by yokels. However, a saying that I found in Joseph Bridge's book on Cheshire proverbs and sayings caught my eye, and just might be connected with Freckleton:—

A whim-wham from Yockleton. If old people are interrupted by inquisitive young ones, asking what they are talking about, this stock phrase is used in reply. It is nonsensical. Of course, there is no Yockleton, in Cheshire nor anywhere else. A local rhyme goes:—

> *Yockleton was Yockleton when 'Pool was but a pup,*
> *An' it'll still be Yockleton when 'Pool is sluthered up.*

'Pool is neighbouring Blackpool, a relatively modern place in the eyes of old Freckleton villagers. Sluthered means "covered in slutch" (muck).

Little America. "Freck" is so close to Warton as to be grafted on to it, or the other way about, so see Warton. The name was given to both townships.

FYLDE

The Fylde is an old word which simply means "the field". **Windmill Land.** This name was coined by Charles Allen Clarke (1863-1935) ("Teddy Ashton") for the area in which, of necessity, there were many windmills. He wrote about the area a great deal, and used the name in his three most popular books—"Windmill Land", "More Windmill Land" and "Windmill Land Stories". He saw it as a place of peace and tranquillity, and wrote:—

> *If you are sad and sick of strife,*
> *If cares and burdens fret your life,*
> *Let Heaven take you by the hand,*
> *And lead you into Windmill Land.*

He also coined the name **"Steam Engine Land"** for the area around his native Bolton.

R.J.B.

The local historian Thornber, writing in 1837, called the area **"The Wheatfield of Amounderness"**. Amounderness is the ancient name for the Hundred of which the Fylde is part. It stretched from the Ribble northwards to the Lonsdale Hundred, and from the Irish Sea eastwards to the Blackburn Hundred.

Favoured by many people as a retirement area, the Fylde, in common with other sea-side spots such as Morecambe, has many elderly residents. Twice the national average is the figure spoken of locally, and because of this the rather unkind nickname of **"Costa Geriatrica"** has been given to the area, making an obvious reference to the various "costas" which exist in Spain.

GALGATE, near Lancaster

Galgate—Rhubarb City. A plant commonly known as "wild rhubarb", which is not even one of the same botanical family but certainly resembles rhubarb, grew and probably still grows, on the railway embankments around Galgate. Visitors from the industrial areas going by rail to Morecambe or the Lake District saw it and associated the township with the plant. A similar story, slightly varied, is to be told about Clifton, Farnworth and Droylsden.

GAYTHORN, Manchester

Little Ireland. An area of Gaythorn (which is part of Hulme) near the place where the Gaythorn Gas Works was situated, and near Oxford Road Railway Station, was so called because a high percentage of the population were of Irish extraction. Housing conditions there were extremely bad. See Sir James Kay-Shuttleworth's work "Moral and physical conditions of the working classes" 1833. The Irish probably moved in during the 1820s and early 1830s, soon after the area was built. There was an area nearby known as **"Irish Town"**—see Aspin, "Lancashire the first Industrial Society" (1969), p. 93. The name can be compared with a similar one for an area of Whitefield, and a modern equivalent at Haslingden.

GLAZEBURY, Manchester

Berry Loaners (or Laners) are inhabitants of the township. Berry Lane was the name of a former town near which Cromwell fought a battle in the Civil War known as the Battle of Berry Lane.

GLODWICK, Oldham

Glodwick Mice. The reason for this nickname is not known, but I suggest that it may refer sarcastically to the timidity of the residents.

A story exists in local lore about the **Glodwick Shamrock Band.** It may well have been that the band had Irish connections, but it was rumoured that some members of the band ate some shamrock, to the delight of non-bandsmen, who coined the name.

GORTON, Manchester

Gorton Bulldogs. The nickname is quoted by FET (1901). I can suggest only one reason for it (other than being simply a term of derision applied to several groups by children—e.g. **Catholic Bulldogs**—and having little to do with British tenacity):— Harland, in CBSL, quotes a song called Gorton Town which was written and sung by John Beswick, alias Parish Jack, on the occasion of the naming of a dog called Ringwood in February 1865 in The Hare and Hounds Inn, Abbey Hey, Gorton. It is not difficult to imagine that if the song was written with a bulldog in mind, the dog's fame would increase each time the song was sung.

GREAT HARWOOD, near Blackburn

Great Harwood is pronounced **Gret 'Arrud** in the dialect. Great Harwood—**Snuffy Arrud** or simply **Snuffy.** This nickname arose from the snuff-taking habit of local people working as mill weavers. The reason for the habit is not known, but it seems to have been passed down through several generations. **Snuffies**— the people of the town. It was said that one could always tell a Harwood weaver from others because his moustache would be stained brown by snuff, although he was equally likely to have chewed "bacca".

A variation on the snuff theme is the legend that there was once a snuff mill in the town. I have found no record of any, though some enterprising person ought to have built one if the habit of the mill workers has not been exaggerated, and I have no reason to think that it has. There is a district of Blackburn called Little Harwood—Little 'Arrud. See Kirkham.

GREEN HAWORTH, near Accrington

Bedlam. A madhouse or scene of an uproar. It is said that, in the days when miners lived in this hillside settlement, each

Saturday they would indulge in excessive drinking and use foul language. The police would attend, and an old sergeant named it **"Bedlam"**. If there is any truth in the story, then it can probably be dated as post-1840. Further research on mining in the area could better fix the date, though boisterous farmers are just as likely to have made the place what it was.

Humbug Land. Some enterprising cottager in the settlement— it is hardly a village—became locally famed for the quality of his humbugs. They became known as **Bedlam Humbugs** and are remembered with great affection by many people still living—see Digby and Miller, "An Accrington Miscellany", p. 24.

HALLIWELL, Bolton

Halliwell—T'City. It truly refers to the Brownlow Fold area of Halliwell. There is a public house called "The City" there. **Spake Aisy.** One part of Halliwell had this name applied to it, probably alluding to the American prohibition era (and possibly coined then) and the large number of public houses there. It was an area "with a pub on every corner".

HASLINGDEN

Sheep Greeners. Sheep Green is part of Haslingden and by usage the name came to be applied to all Haslingden people, in just the same way as Atherton came to be known as Chow Bent. Originally then it would not be a true nickname. **Grane Cuckoos.** "The Grane" or "Haslingden Grane" is a stretch of moorland on the west of the town, a rural part of Haslingden. The nickname was meant to indicate supposed rusticity, and all that that implied to the industrial worker—simplicity, slowness of mind and body.

Haslingden — **T' capital of Asia Minor.** In the 1960s many Pakistanis and Indians came to live in the town to work in the cotton mills. This was experienced by other towns, of course, but the large number gave rise to this nickname. It is possible that similar names on the same theme exist but are not yet recorded. I have heard Bradford in Yorkshire referred to as "Gateway to the East" and Birmingham as "Bangalore". The same traits of humour are evident in such names as are found in these first applied over 100 years ago. Compare with "Little Ireland"—see Whitefield and Gaythorn.

HAUGHTON, Denton

Haughton Boggarts. Boggarts are ghosts and appear frequently in Lancashire folk lore. No doubt there are stories of boggarts in the area around Haughton (not to be confused with Aughton near Ormskirk), and this nickname alludes to those stories. For stories on boggarts, see Hird, "Clayton Hall boggart and Boggart Hole Clough". The nickname is not referred to in Middleton's book "Annals of Hyde", 1899.

HAYDOCK

Yickville and **Yickers.** These two names are given to the township and the inhabitants respectively. They are terms which infer simplemindedness—a hick is an American term for a simpleton —and make use of the "Y" in the word, as is done in "Heywood".

HEATON, Prestwich

Yetton, the local pronunciation—FET. There are three Heatons in Lancashire, one near Morecambe, one near Bolton and this one. I suggest that Taylor meant the Prestwich Heaton because of the South-East Lancashire connection. The pronunciation did not amount to a nickname so far as I am aware but I think it worthy of inclusion.

HEYSHAM

Monkey Town. This is a nickname given by Morecambe fishermen to the township, which is now part of the borough of Morecambe and Heysham. The origin is said to be from the finding of the body of a monkey, probably coming from some ship sailing in Morecambe Bay, which was thought by locals to be human. It is another example of a derogatory term. See Heywood, Sunderland Point and Morecambe. Heysham and Heywood have the same pre-fix, and it may be wondered whether the supposed origin of Heywood (Ape Bridge) bears more than a hint of truth.

HEYWOOD

Heywood is pronounced Yewood in the dialect. Heywood — **Monkeytown.** Irish immigrants coming to the town many years ago, when it was called Heap Bridge, pronounced it Ape Bridge. The "ape" was developed into "monkey" and the place became "Monkey Town". There are other explanations for the origin, such as the story about the flood waters receding away from

Noah's Ark and the occupants disembarking and populating Heywood; also the one of the circus passing through the town and the monkeys escaping, mixing and breeding with the Heywood residents, until the townsfolk themselves came to be known as **Monkey Towners.**

Ringtails. These are a type of monkey, so the inhabitants of Monkey Town gained a more sophisticated name. It is said, too, and this can be verified still, that the public houses in Heywood had holes in the stools so that the monkeys could comfortably place their tails through. That the holes were put there for carrying purposes seems too realistic to be true. They **must** be for monkey tails. The holes were unlikely to be used, as on the Continent, for placing sun umbrellas through. See Heysham. See "The Heywood Advertiser", 29th October, 1933.

In Heywood at some time past was a very tall mill chimney, 195 ft. high, which had a lean to one side. This earned it the local nickname of **"The English Tower of Pisa".**

HIGHER WALTON, part of Walton-le-Dale, near Preston

Moon's Millers. There was an ancient cornmill in Walton-le-Dale, but the mill owned by Mr. Moon was erected late in the 18th century and still stands, being known as Moon's Mill. This is an unusual example of how trade or work in a particular area gained it a nickname. Mannex's Directory of 1854 describes Moon's Mill as "another populous village, with 2 large cotton mills, one of which is very extensive and was erected in 1850 ... the village is situated on the Southern bank of the Darwen, about 3 miles S.E. of Preston."

HINDLEY, near Wigan

Hindley **Bullyeds**, Hindley **Jockyeds**, Hindley **Bluffins**. All three names are derogatory, inferring blockheadedness or stupidity.

HOLLINGWORTH

T'Weyvers' Sayport. Hollingworth Lake gained this name in the 1860s, just before trips to Blackpool became very popular. Excursions were run from the nearby mill towns to the Lake, and advertised by the Lancashire & Yorkshire Railway Company. The day trippers were well catered for at several pubs. There were pleasure gardens and steam-driven roundabouts for the children. There was a steam ferryboat on the water, and at one time the famous Captain Webb could be seen there training for his Channel swims (and thinking about inventing matches, perhaps).

HOLLINWOOD, near Oldham

Hollinwood Ruffyeds (Rough heads). It is solely because of its proximity to Oldham that this name has been applied. See Oldham.

HOOLEY HILL, part of Ashton-under-Lyne

Hooley Hill Shepsters. A shepster is the Old English, and thus dialect, word for starling. I suggest that the people of the area were noted for fine singing, or perhaps that it was a reference to the rural area by those living in industrial parts. It is a rare example of a nickname being based on a bird.

HOPWOOD, Middleton

Hopwood Angels. This nickname probably arises out of a sarcastic irony—the inhabitants were perhaps anything but angelic. However, as this is how nicknames did arise, it is possible that the name hides a feeling of derision, and that the inhabitants were do-gooders or good-living people thought "cissy". It may be the opposite term to "bulldogs"—see Gorton.

HORWICH

Horwich Locos. The name has little to do with the inhabitants being crazy, or "loco" as the Americans say, but a lot to do with the railway industry with which Horwich was and is connected.

The connection started in 1884 when the Lancashire and York-shire Railway Company bought Horwich Estates and other lands at a cost of £36,000 for the 736 acres (£49 per acre). The well-known railway works were opened two years later, and two years after that the Horwich Railway Mechanics' Institute (R.M.I.). The fame of the place in railway circles cannot be overlooked, as by 1895 the works were rated the best in the world. A football club was started on land owned by the Institute for the 1910/11 season. They were nicknamed "The Locos" though they bear the proud name Horwich R.M.I.

Horwich Sleepers. Undoubtedly this is a sarcasm with wit, based on the railway (sleeper) connection and supposed "doziness".

Horwich Sleepers, a jocular term for the inhabitants of Horwich —FET. See Marshall, "The Lancashire and Yorkshire Railway". See "Horwich and Westhoughton Journal", 25.11.1966. Horwich is derived from the Anglo-Saxon, meaning "place of the grey wych-elms". Note its central position in Lancashire, an ideal railway centre.

HUYTON, near Liverpool

I can trace no nickname for Huyton, but it is mentioned in local rhymes:—

> *Prescot, Huyton and merry Childow,*
> *Three parish churches in a row.*

> *Prescot for mugs,* **Huyton for ploydes,**
> *Childow for ringing and singing besides*

("Ploydes" may mean festivities or parties.)

> *Preston for pan mugs,* **Huyton for pride,**
> *Childwall for toiling and playing besides.*

JERICHO, near Bury

In his book "Playtimes in a busy life" (1909), William Trevor, a Manchester man, says: "There is good evidence that it was always called Jericho in the early years of last century, and I am inclined to the conclusion that Jericho is a name of derision, and that someone, not in good odour" (yes, he actually used that word) "would in the first instance, be alluded to as having 'takken Jericho', for Lancashire people are always good at expressing their scorn in a nickname. Hence, the hated workhouse there, 40 or 50 years since, was never alluded to by the poor except as

Bastille." So far as the origin of the town name was concerned, he was on the wrong tack, as it is most likely that the truth is that the Hall family of Boaredge (in Jericho) chose the name for its Biblical connection. In nearby Birtle is a place called Ninevah. His mention of the workhouse is interesting. There is a large hospital, descendant of the workhouse, still in Jericho.

"Go to Jericho" had the same meaning as **"Go to Bootle".** Bath, and Ince near Chester, also figure in the phrase, as does (among others) somewhere called Blazes.

KEARSLEY, near Farnworth

Kaishy Moorites. LBY says the reason for this name is the same reason that Atherton folks are called Cocky Moorites. I believe that he is wrong—see Atherton. However, the name is almost certainly a corruption of Kearsley Moorites, i.e. the people who lived on Kearsley Moor, which is a stretch of moorland above the township.

KIRKHAM

Snuffy and **Snuff and Porter.** These two names are from the same derivation. A local legend refers to a snuff mill once being in the town, but this is not so. However, it is known that in the early 19th century John Birley, the local squire, employed many Irish immigrants in his flax mill, and those operatives had the habit of taking snuff and drinking porter in what little leisure time they had. It was common for North Fylde folk to ask "Weer are ta' gooin?" and to receive the reply, "Ah'm gooin tu Snuff and Porter". This simply meant that the person was going to Kirkham. The phrase was in use in the 1930s, and Kirkham is still referred to as "Snuffy".

It has been suggested that the name arose from the notices displayed outside the beer houses of the town—"Licensed for Ale, Snuff and Porter", but H.M. Customs and Excise librarian says that it is unlikely that the name arose on account of the licensing requirements for these commodities. Whilst some public houses may have displayed such advertising signs, the items were not licensed under those names. Incidentally, there were at one time 22 public houses in Kirkham.

KNUZDEN, near Blackburn

Knuzden—Gobbinland. Whilst it is close to Blackburn, Knuzden also shares a boundary with Oswaldtwistle which is widely known as Gobbinland, and I suggest that that name was applied to Knuzden as being so close to Oswaldtwistle that the boundary did not matter.

LAMBERHEAD GREEN, between Wigan and Orrell

Lomra' Greeners. Not a nickname, but included to show the dialect contraction. **Pig o' th' wallers.** It was said of the inhabitants that they, being "Gawbies", held their pigs up on the top of a wall so that the pigs could see the passing of a band or procession. It is a story repeated to apply to the inhabitants of many Lancashire—and Yorkshire—towns. See Tottington, Unsworth, Winwick.

LANCASHIRE

Lancashire Sprawngers. A sprawnger was a village teller of humorous stories. This then is an allusion to the humour of the Lancastrian. See Hird. **Lancashire—Lanky,** and Lancashire dialect —twang; thus the Lancashire dialect has long been referred to **as " 't Lanky twang".** It is not so much a nickname as a dialect expression.
Lancashire law—No stake, no draw. This is an old saying. It was used to signify that only those who contribute to something can claim a share, or draw, of the whole.
Tim Bobbin. This was the pen name of John Collier (1710— 1786) who wrote and published his humorous works in the Lancashire dialect (and is seen as the "father" of our dialect writers). Since then the term has been applied jocularly to the inhabitants generally of South Lancashire—FET.
Christ's Croft. There is no "Lancashire" mentioned in the Domesday survey. It is called "the land between Mersey and Ribble", and in latter years this area, what we might now call Southern Lancashire, was nicknamed—Baines calls it an "appelation given"—Christis Crofte, or Christ's Croft. It was sparsely populated and was thus a place of some security when other areas were troublesome. A rhyme was used to illustrate this point:—

> *When all England is alofte,*
> *Safe are they that are in Christis Crofte:*
> *And where should Christis Crofte be,*
> *But between Ribble and Mersey.*

It has been suggested, without basis in fact, that Lanca-shire was a corruption of Lancelot-shire, or the shire administered by Sir Lancelot.
Lancashire Witches. Long before William Harrison Ainsworth wrote his famous novel "The Lancashire Witches" (1848), the

county's name had been linked with the ancient craft. In 1602, which was ten years before the trial of the Pendle-area women whose antics have provided interest to this day, one John de Brentford wrote: "The women (of Lancashire) are mostly handsome—and their fascinating manners have long procured for them the name of Lancashire Witches." The first witchcraft trial in Lancashire had been in 1447. In 1634 a play had been acted upon the London stage called "The Late Lancashire Witches", and in 1681 the poet Shadwell produced his play "The Lancashire Witches", which was really a religious drama with Lancashire-speaking characters. Cashing in on the act, a writer called Fitzball produced an opera based on Ainsworth's novel in 1848. The name was here to stay. See Kathleen Eyre's book "Witchcraft in Lancashire" (Dalesman 1974).

Lancashire Lads & Lasses. These names doubtless arose through the ease with which the "L" and the short "a" in both words flow off the tongue. Everyone seems to have enjoyed the name at one time, including soldiers and Gracie Fields. The earliest recorded use of the name is when, on 8th August 1586, there was listed in the Stationer's Hall Register "A new Northern songe of a Lancashire Lad".

In an essay on food, Charles Roeder recorded (1902) that as a nickname, **"Pratapies"** for Lancashire people was not uncommon.

LANCASTER

Time-honoured Lancaster. This northernmost Lancashire city is an ancient place, to which time seems to give added beauty and charm. The Lancaster people are proud of their past and their heritage. Whilst not a nickname, the phrase is comparable only with "Bonny Colne o' th' hill" as being examples of complimentary description.

Gaunt's Pile. This nickname is a reference to the connection which the Castle—built on a pile or hill—has with John o'Gaunt, Duke of Lancaster, son of Edward III. Lancaster is pronounced "Lankistur" in South-East Lancashire—FET (1901).

Whilst I can find no nickname or saying to confirm it, it is certain that in the days before tinned and packeted foods, Lancaster had quite a name for salmon. It was so plentiful that it was customary for appprentices to stipulate in their indentures that they should not be fed on it more than three days a week. Of course, the river Lune is still a favourite with fishermen seeking the salmon.

Lancaster Castle

LEES, near Oldham

Lees Shaftwratchers. To "wratch" is a dialect expression meaning to stretch. A legend tells of a mill engineer who found that the main driving shaft on a machine was too short by a fraction. He mobilised all the machine minders in an effort to pull the shaft, tug-of-war fashion, in order to lengthen it. The nickname can thus be dated as being after the Industrial Revolution, and a 19th century poet, Will o' the Wisp, wrote a poem which includes reference to the story. It is called "The Song of the Shaftwratchers", and begins:—

Come all ye Ashton Rickers, ye Owdham Roofyeds too,
Ye Moonrakers from Middleton, ah'll tell yo summat new.
Ye Ratchda Bacon Makers and ye Bucks fra Monkey teawn,
Come harken heaw the village o' Lees has risen to reneawn.

Chorus:—

Wi' a long poo and a strong poo
Together poo away,
We'll no be beaten bi a shaft,
We'll wratch it once today.

44

This poem is an early record of the use of nicknames. I see the "bucks" not as a nickname but as an expression meaning young, strong men—see Bootle. See Royton. **Lees Shaftwratchers** — a jocular term for the inhabitants of Lees—FET.

Lees Pie-cans. This expression was used by Oldham people to describe Lees folk as idiots. A story is told of a Lees knocker-up who got a new pole with which to go about his trade. It was too long, so he got a cushion to kneel on so that it would shorten his reach.

The Athens of the North. So great was the thirst for knowledge of Lees villagers at some time in its past that this name was dubbed on the place. Edinburgh was similarly named, as was Warrington.

LEIGH

Leigh—Leyth. Leigh folk—**Leythers.** These expressions are used even today with some degree of pride in their town and their dialect by Leigh people. They are strictly not nicknames, but their existence perhaps explains why I have been unable to trace any nicknames applied to the town. There is some degree of Lancashire wit in the expressions, which poke fun at the English spelling and pronunciation.

LITTLE CROSBY

It was said of Little Crosby in the 17th century:— **"That it had no beggars, nor an alehouse, nor a Protestant in it."** Clearly, there must have been some good living, pious, Roman Catholics there.

LITTLE HULTON, near Bolton

Little Hulton Tripehounds. LBY suggests that the name arose because on the main street of the village (as it was some years ago) there were a lot of tripe shops, locally known as "Thripe hoyles". Tripe was there to be eaten "straight from the wood" as it was impaled on wooden skewers. Research has failed to verify or refute the suggestion about the number of shops, which I think was probably exaggerated. However, it is true that the Lancashire tripe trade flourished between 1910 and 1936. A more feasible explanation is that the term is a derogatory one meaning a rather skinny-looking dog, and quite likely to be applied by the Lancastrian. It is true that tripe was sold on wooden skewers.

Tripe is a product of the ox, but pig's tripe is known as maw and is sold in pork-butchers' shops. As a point of interest, there are four main kinds of tripe:— (a) Thick seam—used either in

cooking or to be eaten cold; (b) honeycomb—best used in cooking; (c) black or leaf—eaten cold or fried; and (d) beef or weasand
—solid meat, eaten cold or can be minced. Tripe was served on
golden salvers as a delicacy in Roman feasts, over 2,000 years
ago.

LITTLEMOSS, part of Droylsden

Poker-knob town. This name arose from the habit of locals of
knocking on the fire-back, in the days of coal fires in terraced
houses, with a poker to attract the attention of the next-door
neighbour.

LIVERPOOL

Probably Liverpool people, with their quick wits, sarcastic
comments and lively humour have created more local nicknames
than others. Many have been short-lived and not in general use,
and perhaps for these reasons among others I have not yet heard
of them.

Scousers. A favourite dish of the Liverpudlian has long been
"lobscouse" which is a form of potato hash. The name has
become contracted to "scouse" and applied to the Liverpudlian.
It came into general use after the First World War.

Frisby Dyke. A company of drapers trading under this name
(Frisby Dyke Ltd.) was founded in Liverpool in 1850 and
liquidated in 1936. The name was used for a character played in
the radio programme ITMA by Deryck Guyler in the Second
World War. The popularity of the programme was such that the
character came to be thought to be the epitome of a Liverpudlian
and any Liverpudlian (outside Liverpool) was to be called Frisby
Dyke. The name is now little used.

Liverpool Gentlemen. This phrase should be read along with
those of "Manchester men" and others to show the subtle
difference of each, particularly of the Liverpudlian. I have traced
several versions of the phrase and quote them:—

"Salford lads, Manchester men, Liverpool gentlemen" (described by Wainwright in "Liverpool Gentlemen: a history of
Liverpool College", as an ironical Lancashire catch-phrase).

"Liverpool gentlemen, Manchester man, Houdham chap and
a Rachdill felly".

A coachman is said to have remarked, when asked about his
passengers: "A gen'leman from Liverpool, a man from Manchester, a fella from Wigan and a chap from Bowten", also, "A
gentleman fro' Liverpool, a mon fro' Manchester, a chap fro'
Owdham and a felly fro' Wigan." See "Notes and Queries", series
6, vol. 3, 1881, and series 12, vol. 8, 1921. Also see Arthur Lay-

cock's "Warren of Manchester" in which there is a story "Liverpool Gentlemen, Manchester Men and Owdham Chaps". **Liverpool gentlemen**—a sarcastic term used in contradistinction to Manchester Man—FET. I believe that this is the mostly likely explanation of the nickname arising.

Dicky Sam. This is a very old term for a Liverpudlian, usually applied to a person who was born in the old parish of Liverpool, near Mann Island. **Liverpudlian.** A puddle is of course a small pool of water, so coining this nickname, now in quite common and respectable use, would be an easy matter, as it would be in "Blackpudlian" (see Blackpool).

The Mersey Funnel. The very shape of the tunnel, opened in 1934, suggests a funnel or tube, and Liverpudlians were not slow to see the similarity of the two words. The much more recent Second Mersey Tunnel was named **"The Mersey Mousetrap"** by a local newspaper, and the construction company were reputed to dislike the name. **Paddy's Wigwam.** The Liverpool Metropolitan Cathedral's modern design was thought by the city's public to be comical as well as conical, and this gave them licence to "christen" it in this way.

Speke Castle. In the mid-1970s, an adventure playground was constructed by the local council for Speke children. It resembles a fortification, and was probably intended to look that way. I like to think that the local children created this nickname, and not the journalist from whom I heard it.

The Dockers' Umbrella was the name given to the now defunct Overhead Railway.

Whackers. A matey term first used by Liverpudlians to each other, then applied as a nickname to them by others. Taylor equates it with "Quaker", but now everyone knows it is derived from words meaning "to share or divide". When pea soup was distributed free to the poor, it was known locally as "pea whack".

Incidentally, a "dicky sam" was the name given to the peaked, silk hat worn by firemen on ocean liners sailing out of Liverpool in the days of coal-burners, and the Liverpool historian Picton said that the name should be applied only to one born within earshot of the bells of the parish church of St. Nicholas. It has been said too that the name means "Small Yank". Sam of course is a nickname for an American, and dicky is a slang word for little. Think of dicky bird.

Liverpolitan is a posh, Latinised term which means Liverpudlian.

Scousetown. Writing in the Journal of the Lancashire Dialect Society (1958-60), local writer Frank Shaw said that there was then no justification for reserving this name for the area around Scotland Road. It should be applied to the whole city.

The whole city was (and is) referred to with pride by dwellers

47

therein as **"The Pool"**. Those people certainly showed their humour when they (especially tram conductors) referred to that area of the city called Old Swan as **"The Ancient Duck"**. I can't yet discover the reason for their calling the Juvenal Street area "Sevastopol".

LOWER BROUGHTON, Salford

Herring Town   LBY suggests that the name is an allusion to the favourite food of the townsfolk   It may be so, though any herrings eaten would be "imported" from the coastal ports. I think they would be a cheap dish even so, and thus popular. It is another example of foodstuffs coming into use in a nickname.

LOWTON

Lowten (pronounced **Loten**) **Sparrows.**   LBY suggests that the name arose because the people were so very ordinary. This strikes me as a reasonable explanation.

LUMB IN ROSSENDALE

Sad Cake Land.   Lumb shares this name with other Rossendale villages. It is believed to have arisen from the liking of the inhabitants for the food. See Waterfoot, and see Digby, "Rossendale Anthology".

I am indebted to the Catering Dept. of the Blackpool College of Technology for the recipe for sad cake:— 1 lb. plain flour, $\frac{1}{4}$ oz. salt, 8 oz. finely grated suet (there must be no skin), 5 oz. cold water, mix to a dough and bake on flat tin. An alternative method is to change the suet for lard. Try it with jam on, or better still warm with best butter—"real tack". "Sad" simply means heavy, and is brought about by the lack of yeast to raise it. The term is applied even to fruit cake which fails to rise.

LYTHAM ST. ANNES

The two townships of Lytham and St. Annes were amalgamated in 1922. **Sand-grown 'un.** Any locally born person is known as a sand-grown 'un, although a good deal of the soil of the town is fertile peaty loam. The name possibly was brought by the fishermen who came to populate the area from the Southport area, although the name could well have been in use before the early 19th century, when the coastal area began to be populated.
Opal of the West.   St. Annes was a totally new town, built on virgin soil. It was the idea, brought to fruition, of a small num-

ber of Rossendale men who saw the commercial possibilities of housing development there and thought it was a "jewel" of a town. The nickname may have been coined as a commercial catch-phrase but it came into general use.

Golden Land. Charles Allen Clarke came up with this name, doubtless of his own invention, in his book "Windmill Land". He could see only sunny days in Lytham, or, as it is still known locally, **"Leafy Lytham"**.

In his novel of Blackpool theatre life of 1938, "Leading Lady" (1947), D. L. Murray wrote a little rhyme that I'm not so sure the residents of Lytham would have approved of. They have a reputation, earned perhaps by a few but certainly not by the majority, of being "toffee-nosed".

Oh, Douglas has its Ramsay, its Laxey, and its Peel,
But give me dear old Lytham, with its trotters and cow-heel.
Oh, Brighton has its Regent, its Pavilion and its Dome,
But Lytham, dear old Lytham, is the sweetest home-from-home.

See Eyre, "Sand Grown", also "Fylde Folk, Moss or Sand"; Ashton, "Lytham"; Harrison, "Rage of Sand".

When I lived in St. Annes in the early 1960s, there was a council house estate nicknamed **"Mau Mau Territory"** perhaps because of the supposed fierceness of the natives or because it was some distance from the rest of the town. This illustrates the continuance into present-day use of nicknames.

MANCHESTER

Manchester Men. A playful contradistinction to Liverpool Gentlemen—FET. For more on this, see Liverpool. It is intended to be sarcastic. **"The Manchester Man"**. Not a nickname, but the title of a novel by Mrs. G. Linnaeus Banks. It has recently been reprinted. **Manchester bred, long i' th'arms and short i' th'head.** This is a saying connected with Manchester people.

To illustrate that the Lancastrian practice of giving nicknames is not dead, I have recorded one right up-to-the-minute, as fresh as 1976. Central Manchester's new Arndale Centre is not yet, as I write, completed, but most of its façade is covered in yellowish (intended to be sandstone-coloured) tiles. The locals have named it **"Superloo"** and **"The biggest public toilet in Europe"**.

MARTON, Blackpool

Marton Mossogs. Marton Moss is now noted as a market garden area, with black peaty soil. It has been drained since originally being a moss, but is still known as "t'Moss". Thus the inhabitants are known as Mossogs, a very simple term meaning Mossites.

Moss Ullerts or Ullets. The reason for the name is not easy to fix, as the name could have arisen through several reasons: (a) Ullet means owl. Also hullet, hullert, ulyet, ullert—FET. Thus the name may allude to the wisdom of the people. The term ullet meaning owl was in use in the Fylde in 1837. (b) Tullet means small gull. This was in use in 1837, and could well have been a common bird on the Moss. (c) Ullert—a child's name for a large moth or butterfly; it is also a contemptuous name for a vulgar, ill-behaved woman—FET.

I suggest that the "wise owl" derivation is the most likely, though many Moss folk were thought anything but wise. A delightful story to illustrate this concerns the first clock ever brought on to the Moss. It was wheeled round in a barrow, and when folk asked what it was they were told by the "sages" that it was something called a "Tickmajig" which would destroy the nation, marking the end of the world. They treated it with the contempt it deserved by throwing stones at it.

It was said, too, that Moss folk were so daft that they did not know what day it was, and had to have a bellman round to let them know when Sunday approached, by shouting "Once more dark, then Sunday." The call is certainly true, as this was called by the bellman acting for the Squire at Lytham. See Ashton, "Lytham", and Eyre, "Fylde Folk: Moss or Sand".

MELLOR, near Blackburn

Mellor Bull Beef and Skallions. Mellor is an agricultural area on the outskirts of the East Lancashire industrial belt, so a nickname connected with agriculture is not out of place. It could be said that the name is more connected with food than with agriculture, and so would be in common with other nicknames. A skallion is a contraction of skally onion, which means a young onion. Mark Twain's young Huckleberry Finn was often addressed as a "rapscallion" by his negro comrade.

Mellor poots (for pullets). Some doubt exists on whether this nickname refers to Mellor (Blackburn) or to the Mellor in North-West Derbyshire, close to Stalybridge. LBY refers to the nickname as a term of endearment, saying that a Mellor mother would call her child "My pretty poot". It is a name for the inhabitants of Mellor—FET. The contrast between this term of endearment and the term of derision referred to in Aspull Moor Poots is interesting.

MIDDLETON

Middleton Moonraker. Legend tells of several Middleton men trying to fish or rake out of a river or canal what they think is an enormous cheese. It is in fact the moon's reflection. The origin of the story is lost, as it has been passed down by word of mouth. In the "Ring o'Bells" hotel in Middleton is a large oil painting depicting the scene of the incident. It bears the legend: "It's theer mon, rake it eawt."

The story varies little from the legends recalled by the Wiltshire Moonraker and the Slaithwaite (Yorkshire) Moonraker. At these two places, the "fishermen" were not so simple as their Middleton counterparts, as they were fishing for the moon as a pretence to fool the excise men, since they were in fact searching for brandy kegs known to be in the river. The ruse worked, but if it worked a second time is not recorded. See Lees.

MILNROW, near Rochdale

Milnrow—**Mildrow** in the dialect—FET. **Milnrow Painters.** A story exists of a hoax perpetrated on some men at Milnrow by a man who, in a period of unemployment, promised them work on painting the railway station provided that they brought their own paint brushes. When they turned up, of course, the station master knew nothing about it. They had been "had". Similar stories of hoaxes are told all over Lancashire. The name is shared by Newhey people. Newhey is part of Milnrow Urban District.

The Rochdale poet Harvey Kershaw has written a poem on the subject.

MITTON

No nicknames are applied to Mitton or its inhabitants. Several rhymes concern the village and its connection with three Lancashire rivers. One of them is:—

> *The Hodder, the Calder, the Ribble and Rain*
> *All meet at a point in Mytton's domain.*

Mitton is interesting both to the Lancastrian and to the Yorkshire Tyke because the two counties, despite what Whitehall may have told us recently, meet there. Great Mytton was "white rose" and Little Mytton red. You will have noticed variations in spelling. The most authoritative of the local historians use the "i", but it is true to say that both "i" and "y" are used.

MORECAMBE

Morecambe was formerly called Poulton-le-Sands, and it is the sands which gave rise to a nickname. **Sand-grown 'un.** This term describes a person who was born in or around Morecambe. It should be compared with similar nicknames for other Lancashire coastal areas from Mersey to Lune.

Writing in the 1920s, John Randal Swann called Morecambe **"The Golden Gate to Lakeland"**. He was not a writer likely to initiate the use of such a name, more likely to have recorded its use by other people. In the 1924 Official Guide Book, Morecambe was described as **"The Gateway to Lakeland"** and **"The English Bay of Naples"**.

I don't think that it's there now, but certainly until the late 1960s there was a small park in the centre of Morecambe close to the Ribble bus terminus named **"Dicky Bird Park"** by the locals. I suppose they went there to see the birds. Certainly there were a lot of men there when I went, and plenty of young ladies too.

"The Shrimps". The town's football team gains this nickname from the delicacy for which the town has become far famed, and a pub there bears the name.

MOSSLEY

Mossley Gawps, Mossley Gawbies. Both these terms are derived from "gaby" meaning simpleton. In the dialect, to gawp means to stand and stare, as would a simpleton, and the two terms are synonymous. See Shaw and others.

Bow-Leg Town. Mossley is set among hills, and the majority of its streets are very steep. The inference is that people walking up the streets became bow-legged after a time. The name was in use in the early 1960s. Mossley—**Mawsley: FET.**

MUSBURY, Haslingden

Musbury Turks. In the early 19th century the people of the area were so called because they were allegedly of a rough, infidel type. The advent of Sunday Schools and Chapel broke this image. The phrase was used by Mr. James Stott when laying a foundation stone at a Wesleyan Chapel in Helmshore in 1866. Musbury was absorbed into the Helmshore area of Haslingden about 1870. A local hill is known as Musbury Tor. The similarity between Tor and Turk is interesting but I think the earlier explanation for the nickname rules out the suggestion that "Turk" is a corruption of "Tor". — See Aspin, "Lancashire, the First Industrial Society", p. 109.

NELSON

Seedhillers. The area of Nelson where the town football club ground lies is called Seedhill. The "h" is silent. It seems certain that the nickname arose through the football team, as did several others.

Little Moscow, Muscovites. These two names undoubtedly arose from the strong political fervour of the townsfolk, being well to the Left. The names probably arose in the 1920s. It is suggested that the reason for the names being applied concerns the decision of Richard Winterbottom when he was Mayor of Nelson (1929 to 1931) not to allow the National Anthem to be played at functions he attended. There was from the early 1920s a large, active branch of the Communist Party in the town.

Nelson Clockers. In a poem published in 1905, Teddy Ashton refers to this nickname, but its origin appears to be lost. The only reason that I can suggest is that the workpeople would always "clock" on and off when starting and finishing work in the mills of the town. Another suggestion is that the name may have been mis-heard for "cloggers", indicating that the townsfolk wore clogs, and the football team were what has become known as "physical". It is strange too that a clock features in a saying connected with Colne, Nelson's inseparable sister.

NEWCHURCH IN ROSSENDALE

Kirk.   There has been a church here since ancient times, founded because the Rossendale Valley folk found it difficult to walk to the mother church at Clitheroe. Thus it became the "New" church. The local football team, Rossendale F.C., has the same nickname applied to it. See Newbiggin, "History of the Forest of Rossendale".

NEWHEY, Milnrow

Newhey Painters—see Milnrow.

NEWTON HEATH, Manchester

Botany Bay.   A writer at the turn of the century suggested that Botany Bay, in Newton Heath, was so called because some houses there were built in the same year (1770) that Captain Cook discovered Botany Bay.

NORTHMOOR, Oldham

Northmoor Fiddlers.   The people of Northmoor were formerly reputed to be fine musicians. Two hundred and fifty fiddlers attended the burial of William Barnes, a famous conductor, at St. Paul's Church, Royton, in 1843. I am assured that the nickname has nothing to do with fiddling as connected with dishonesty. The musical connection merits reference to the name applied to the people of Dean in Rossendale.

Northmoor Goslings.   There has been an inn called "The Gaping Goose" at Northmoor for many years, at least since the 1850s, and as it would be the centre of village life at some time, perhaps the nickname infers that the villagers are children of the Goose. The nickname may be compared, however, with that applied to the folk from neighbouring Sholver—Sholver Poots, or pullets. Perhaps one was coined to contradict the other, as both are connected with domestic fowl.

OLDHAM

Oldham is pronounced **"Owdham"**. The term is jocularly substituted for "hell", as in **"Will ah Owdham as like"** and **"It's played Owdham wi'me"**—FET.

Owdham Ruffyeds (Rough heads): There are two possible derivations of the nickname:— (a) Oldhamers wore piled hats made of rough material, and Oldham was a centre for the hatting industry.

(b) Oldhamers were noted for being pugnacious or rough in their habits. A modern equivalent is "roughnecks". This is verified in the diaries of Edwin Butterworth who in 1853 called on the electors of Oldham to "advance if you wish once and for all to abolish your rude and unsightly title of rough heads". In 1834 Butterworth had written, "I am a native of Oldham and consequently a thoroughbred rough head, as my brother townsmen have long been called". The name was applied to the inhabitants of other villages now situated in the Oldham Borough boundary. **Owdham Brewis.** This nickname is quoted by Samuel Bamford in "Early days". Brewis was once a popular dish, a mixture of black puddings and chopped onion with oatcake soaked in water that had been used to boil the other ingredients. S. W. Partington defines it as "an oatmeal drink", so it seems that it could be eaten or drunk, depending upon consistency. There is a saying:—

> *In Oldham brewis, wet and warm,*
> *And Rochdale puddings, there's no harm.*

It is yet another example of a local dish becoming so well known that its name was used as a nickname. **Brewis or Breawis** —Oatcake soaked in hot broth or fat seasoned with pepper and salt.—FET.
Bi th'Owdham—an equivocal oath, probably a corruption of "By the Old 'un" (i.e. the devil)—FET.
Oldham, land of hills and bow-legged women. I heard this phrase from one of the Oldham Tinkers, a trio of singers who help preserve all that is Lancashire. He heard it from a lady in a nearby town, and we assume that it was in general use up to the 1950s. See Mossley for the connection between hills and bow-legs.

I recently came across an old saying which must have some connection with the brewis, which the Welsh call "brywis". It is:—

> *Oatmeal porridge twice a day*
> *Keeps the doctor miles away.*

From Oldham's Clegg Street Station ran the local train that served the Oldham satellite townships to the east which was known as **The Delph Donkey.**

OPENSHAW

Constable of Openshaw sets beggars in the stocks at Manchester. Used in 1670, this phrase poked fun at the folk of Openshaw then a township separate from Manchester, which was 3½ miles away. The Manchester stocks were outside the Cathedral and though beggars could be locked up more locally, at a saving in costs and time, they were taken this distance. Bridge regards it as a Cheshire saying, perhaps because Openshaw was once in the Diocese of Chester. He regarded the explanation as rather unsatisfactory. It would be difficult to think of another.

ORMSKIRK

Ormskirk Gingerbreads. Ormskirk has had a market for many years, and in past centuries gingerbreads would be bought there until the town market became famous for these delicacies, which are similar to gingersnaps. This provides an example of a food-stuff becoming so well connected with a town that its name came to be applied as a nickname. **Ginscake,** a dialect expression meaning gingerbread—FET. **Brandysnaps**, ginger bread cakes sold at fairs—FET.

This ditty was sung in Ormskirk in the 1870s, possibly earlier:—

> *Ormskirk is a funny little town*
> *And long ago was said*
> *To be celebrated for old maids*
> *As well as gingerbread.*

The old maids referred to are those mentioned in the local tradition that the church was erected at the expense of two local maiden ladies called Orm, who couldn't make up their minds whether it should have a tower or a steeple, so they agreed that it should have both.

Ormskirk Heeler. This is not a nickname, but one given to a type of dog bred locally. It is a terrier with black and tan markings. Heeler is a universal term for dogs of this type. They are kept close to heel when not being used for sport or the tending of cattle.

ORRELL, near Wigan

Far Moor End Little Hommers. The Far Moor End area of the town gave rise to this name. Until the 1930s the main industry there was staple and nail making. A tool used in this industry was a small hammer, known as a little hammer in contrast to a big hammer. It is interesting that such a small industry should have two town nicknames connected with it—see Atherton.

OSWALDTWISTLE

Ozzy. This nickname is simply a contraction of the town's full name, and is still in everyday use.

Gobbinland. A gobbin is a slow, dim-witted person, a simpleton. It is a similar expression to "gawby". Local tradition has it that a true Gobbinlander is one who lives "above t' lamp". This lamp is, alas, now no more. It stood near to where the present library is, and was erected in the 1860s in one of the early acts of the newly-formed Local Board. In the first edition of this book, I misplaced the lamp and got hauled over the coals for it. And me an Accrington lad! In Cheshire, there is an area on the north shore of the Dee which was known as Gobbinshire.

The very name of Oswaldtwistle has for many years been a music hall joke, and it is said that a serious effort was in the past made by some townsfolk to change the name. A true Gobbinlander would never allow this.

Another possible explanation of the origin of Gobbinland is that, in the times when small coal mines were operative in the area, the waste from them was taken from the area known as "the gob", which lies in front of the coal face being worked. There would be plenty of tips of this gob-waste, so the name "Gob-land" might arise. I think this explanation is less likely to be original than the more generally accepted "simpleton" one.

The Ozzy-born journalist, Mackenzie Porter, who became columnist on the Daily Sketch and editor of a top Canadian newspaper described his home town in a novel (I almost put navel) way. He called it **"the Umbilicus of the Motherland"**.

OVER RIBBLE (from the Northern bank)

The area across the River Ribble viewed from the Northern bank in the Freckleton to Lytham area was known, and indeed still is, as "Over Ribble". In exactly the same manner the area across the River Wyre from Fleetwood is known as **"Over Wyre"**.

Over Ribble Rattens. This term means "Rats" and shows a suffix at one time commonly used to show the plural. It was used in the Fylde in 1837. It may be that the term shows the wit of the Lancashire people in subtly hinting at the river rat whilst calling someone by an unpleasant name. See Freckleton. See Thornber, "Historical and descriptive account of Blackpool and its Neighbourhood", 1837.

OVER WYRESDALE, near Lancaster

Wewwy, or Wewwyland. This nickname, limited in use to the immediate area, was coined to contrast with "Pewwy"—Dolphinholme. It was popular in the 1920s. There was a friendly rivalry between the two villages which developed into mischief when lads of the two settlements got together. See Schofield, "History of Wyresdale".

The river from which the township takes its name is mentioned in a saying, **"As safe as Wyre".** I know of no basis for the saying, and indeed where the river meets the sea, at Fleetwood, the river is particularly unsafe. Perhaps therein lies the meaning.

PADIHAM

Padiham Thicknecks. This phrase was fairly common in the early part of this century, but is little used now. It is a term of derision, possibly meaning "thick from the neck up". **Padjamers.** Thornber wrote of the Padiham people who visited Blackpool en masse that they were distinguished by the particular colour of their stockings. The similarity of the name with "pyjamas" may have had some bearing on the nickname. These Padihamites were probably the first organised trippers to Blackpool, travelling by waggons after having saved up weekly to enable them to take a holiday.

Padiham Rednecks. "Rednecks" is the name commonly given to Roman Catholics, and I think that its application to Padiham people may have some similar connection.

Though I haven't been able to verify, it has been suggested to me that Padiham people were also called **Watterwalkers** for just the same reasons as were Burnley folk.

PENDLEBURY

Pendlebury Purrers. To "purr" is to "kick or punce". A type of fighting, common throughout industrial Lancashire, is placed on record in this name. Men fought "purring" matches wearing clogs (of course—the common footwear) and it was said in an 1836 newspaper that fighting "Lancashire style, i.e. kicking and throttling" was common in the county. Fights would be of two types:— (a) "all in" in which the opponents could kick each other on any part of the body, or (b) "fair" in which kicks were restricted to the body below the knee. The phrase, **"Feyt furr"** (Fight fairly) would be heard from the crowd watching the sport.

Convictions for manslaughter must have been common after these fights. Before 1822, men could be burned in the hand for the offence, but after that such punishment was illegal, and "transportation" and "hard labour" were resorted to. Boltonians, too, were noted for their prowess at "purring". See LL. Other phrases used in connection with this sport were: (a) **Up an' deawn feyt**—a fight in which both hands and feet were used; (b) **Clog-toe pie,** a jocular term for a good kicking; and (c) **Arbitrators**—clogs.—FET.

PENWORTHAM

Penwortham—Bunnocks; and Penwortham folk are "bunnocks". No one seems to know why the township is so called. Locals argue that the name refers to a part of Penwortham known as Lower Penwortham, now called Middleforth, and the folk of that part. It could have some relation to the meaning of "bunnock" used locally as a cake made of oatmeal and treacle, similar to parkin. Having seen that nicknames arising out of local delicacies were applied in other parts of the country, I see no reason why this nickname should not have arisen similarly. In 1837, Thornber defined a bunnock as "a roll of bread" and bunnocks were made and eaten in the Fylde, which is not far away from Penwortham.

Anyone wishing to know more about bannock, bunnocks and indeed most foods consumed by our ancestors would be well advised to read the excellent essay by Charles Roeder "Notes on Food and Drink in Lancashire and other Northern Counties" in the Transactions of the Antiquarian Society of Lancashire & Cheshire (1902). He makes no mention of treacle when speaking of bannock, from which bunnock is derived, but this may mean only that the adding of treacle, if in fact it was added at all—we don't know for sure—was simply a local variation of the recipe. A "bannuc" is first mentioned in the year 1000.

PILLING

There are no nicknames for Pilling or its inhabitants, but it is mentioned in several sayings and proverbs:— (a) **Never done— like Pilling Moss.** This perhaps alludes to the extent of the Mossland, a large area of black peaty soil, or its continual movement. (b) **God's Grace, like Pilling Moss, is endless.** (c)—

> **Once a wood, then a sea,**
> **Now a moss, and e'er will be.**

This rhyme tells of the natural changes that have taken place in Pilling over the years, caused by the incursions of the sea.
T'Pilling Pig. This was the name that the locals gave to the little train which used to run from Knott End to Garstang. Many tales

are told of its rural passengers and operators. See "Garstang and Knott End Railway Book" by Rush and Price, 1964. The stretch between Garstang and Pilling operated from 1870 to 1963, the stretch from Pilling to Knott End from 1908 to 1950. Another brief history is by Frank S. Walmesley in "The Railway Magazine" for December, 1959.

POULTON-LE-FYLDE

There are no nicknames applied to this township or its people, which was a thriving port and market town long before Fleetwood and Blackpool, its neighbours. The word is pronounced **"Pooton"** in the local dialect.

Keep out of Hell and Poulton. This phrase was in common use last century when Poulton was a market town having many more public houses in the town centre than it has now. The people attending the cattle market would drink there, and become disorderly in the town afterwards. A similar phrase is quoted relating to "Hell, Hull and Halifax" in Yorkshire.

Writing in 1837, the local historian Thornber said that Poulton had been formerly known, on account of its commercial importance, as **"the metropolis of the Fylde"**.

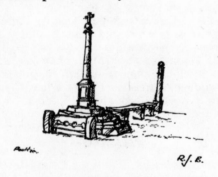

R.J.B.

PRESCOT

Prescot Cables. This nickname almost certainly arose when the local industry of wire and cable making became well known. In 1929 a local cable-making company gave a 1500-seat grandstand to the town football club, and the name of the team was changed to "Prescot Cable", thus ensuring the continuance of the name. See Warrington. **The Alps.** This is the nickname given to the Mines Avenue/Sutherland Road area of Prescot, which has the reputation of being one of the coldest places in the town because of the prevailing wind striking there.

The Blue City. The housing estate around the Cable Road area of the town was called "The Blue City" because at one time all the houses were painted blue. This name and the previous one are examples of nicknames being applied locally through the wit of the inhabitants themselves. See Bury for another example of area nickname application. Prescot is mentioned in two place-rhymes:—

> *Prescot, Huyton and Childow (Childwall),*
> *Three parish churches in a row.*

> *Prescot for mugs, Huyton for ploydes,*
> *Childow for ringing and singing besides.*

"Ploydes" is thought to mean "parties" or "festivities", but may mean "ploughs".

> *Prescot for pan mugs, Huyton for pride,*
> *Childwall for toiling and playing besides.*

Pan mugs were large earthenware vessels which for a long time were manufactured in and around Prescot.

PRESTON

Proud Preston. The origin of this name is lost, but it has been in use for several hundred years, certainly before 1758. Writing then in his "History of the Rebellion", Ray said the place "was vulgarly called Proud Preston on account of its being a place of best fashion. Preston was unexcelled for the politeness of its inhabitants." It has been suggested that Preston was called proud because of its history and importance as the administrative capital of Lancashire.

Dodwell, not the most authoritative of writers, suggests that Preston was first called "proud" because of the ladies of the town who would not "ally themselves with those in trade and did not possess sufficient fortunes for gentlemen". Then he goes on to flatter Preston ladies—"most attractive in appearance and gentle in demeanour".

P.P. In the town's coat of arms is shown a lamb holding a banner. At the base of the shield are the letters "P.P.". Examination of the town's coats of arms of past times reveals that the shield was once a different shape, and moreover that there used to be three "Ps". It is often suggested that "P.P." simply means "Proud Preston", or perhaps "Princeps-Pacis", a Latin motto meaning "Prince of Peace". However, a town historian, Albert Wade, writing in 1940 stated: "There can be little doubt that the letter 'P' stands for Preston and is repeated for ornamentation or to render the design more effective and artistic." This is the view of the majority of town historians. The town seal attached to the Roll of Preston Guild of 1415 has three "Ps", and this is thought to refute the Proud Preston and Princeps-Pacis arguments.

There is a rhyme, which is said to be of contempt for the religious devotion of the townsfolk in the riotous days of revelry (SWP) and which gives some indication of the religious fervour of the townsfolk. At various times in history, Preston has been a centre of Roman Catholicism and of Temperance. The rhyme is:—

> *Proud Preston, poor people.*
> *Eight bells in a cracked steeple.*

This rhyme, varied slightly, is found in various places in Lancashire and Yorkshire. See Ashton and Failsworth.

Preston Nake-necks. This term referring to the collarless, thus naked, necks of the people, is an allusion to poverty (LBY).

Preston Pons. I have traced several authorities to verify the use of this nickname, but cannot positively ascertain the reason for the name. "Pon" is the dialect word for "pan", but so far as can be ascertained, no pan-making industry has existed in Preston The name may have been confused with Prescot Pan Mugs.

In Scotland is a town called Prestonpans, which has no connection historically with our Preston, except that battles were fought at both places in the '45 Rebellion. The Latin word "pons" means "bridge", and Preston's importance as a town has a lot to do with its bridges over the Ribble. Perhaps a simple explanation is that the Lancashire folk looking for a nickname to call Prestonians simply fitted words of little meaning to "P.P."!

The Canary Isles/or Islands. Just south of the "North End" football ground are some streets of terraced houses, each of which is named after a bird—Plover, Wren, Linnet, Goldfinch and so on. It wouldn't take Prestonians long to come up with this nickname, I'm sure. I suggest that it was first used in the late 19th century. By the 1970s the area had become inhabited largely by Asian immigrants, and so was created another nickname for the same area—**"Little India".**

Once Every Preston Guild. This is probably the most common saying connected with a specific township. Everyone knows that Preston Guilds are held every 21 years, and thus anything that is infrequent evokes this saying.

In official meetings, a toast was used in Preston—of course, it begins with a "P"—**Prosperation to the Corporation.**

RADCLIFFE

Radcliffe Boiler Lifters. It is said that in one of the factories in Radcliffe, a gawmless worker was ordered to "shift yon boiler", so he got inside it in order to lift it. It compares with the story of the Lees shaft wratchers.

RAMSBOTTOM

Ramsbottom Rams. The term must have some connection with the name of the town, and is probably just a contraction of the name. A ram is shown in the town coat of arms. **Tup's Arse.** The speech of folk when the Lancashire dialect was much more widely used than it is today enabled the phrase "Ram's bottom" to be converted into everyday language, a little coarse but containing that essence of humour that the Lancastrian loves.

RAWTENSTALL

Rawtenstall Pop-Balls. The sign to indicate a pawnbroker's shop has long been the hanging of three gilt balls outside his shop. LBY suggests that the reason for this nickname being applied was that there were at one time five pawn (called "pop") shops in the town. This cannot be verified and the name does not seem to have been widely used.

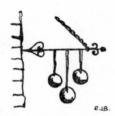

Gun Cottonopolis. The humorist Bernard Hollowood coined this name in an article in Punch about 1944, presumably after a visit there. Very probably gun-cotton was manufactured in Rawtenstall (Rottenstall for the benefit of non-Lancastrian readers) but only Holloway seems to think that she was famous for it. Clearly, he has used a nickname for Manchester as basis for his creation.

Rawtenstall Haymakers. This isn't a nickname, but the name popularly given to a hymn tune "Rawtenstall" by local man John Lord in the late 18th century. In other hymn books, it is called "Bristol" and "Josiah".

RIBCHESTER

A saying relating to Ribchester is:— **"It is written upon a wall in Rome, Ribchester was as rich as any town in Christendom".** Ribchester's connection with Rome is its position as a Roman military encampment. To find out more about this, I suggest a visit to the Roman Museum at Ribchester. The saying was recorded by the historian Fuller in 1662.

RINGLEY, near Bolton

Ringley Broth. The Bolton humorist J. T. Staton wrote a story of this name about a husband who stayed at home one Sunday morning rather than listen to a particular parson at Ringley Chapel. He decided to make broth for dinner, using something he took to be celery tops. The resulting potion smelled and tasted "fow", since it transpired he had used angelica percil.

RIVINGTON

If Rivington Pike do wear a hood
Be sure that day will ne'er be good.

This is a saying recorded by Bridge and is just one of many sayings throughout the country which link hills and weather. Another Cheshire writer, Leigh, recorded the name as "Riving Pike" (1856).

Local historian Thomas Hampson records two more local rhymes:—

Sweet Rivington, or Riventon, thou art a lovely place,
In every hill, in every dale, some beauty we may trace.

*   *   *

When Rivington puts on her hood
She fears a rainy day.
But when she doffs it you will find
The rain is o'er and still the wind
And Phoebus shines away.

Hampson tells us that, at various times in history, her name has been Rovington, Riventon and Rivenpike.

ROCHDALE

Rochdale Bacon Makers. This nickname is mentioned in a poem (see Lees) and undoubtedly refers to the times before Rochdale was the thriving industrial centre it has been for so long, when pig-keeping would be carried on by many people. **Rachda fellas.** In the dialect, Rochdale is pronounced "Rachda" and this was a "jocular term for the inhabitants of Rochdale"—FET. See Liverpool.

Rochdale Insects. This name is obviously connected with the "Hornets"—the Rugby League Club. **Rochdale Bulldogs.** The reason for this name being first applied may be connected with a tenacity of the townsfolk, but I suggest that it is simply a derogatory term. See Gorton.

Rochdale Rush-bearers. This nickname dates back to the time when English villages made holiday when collecting the rushes that they would use in churches to place on the floor as mats and carpets. A Lancashire poet, Elijah Ridings, wrote a verse about rush-bearing and Morris dancing:—

> *Behold the rush cart in the throng*
> *Of lads and lasses pass along;*
> *Now watch the nimble Morris dancers,*
> *Those blithe, fantastic antic prancers.*

> *Bedecked with gaudiest profusion,*
> *Of ribbons in a gay confusion*
> *Of brilliant colours, richest dyes*
> *Like wings of moths and butterflies.*

See LL and Hird for much on rush-bearing.

Rochdale Mashers. A "masher" is today called a "smasher", and means a "toff" or "dandy". See Ashton-under-Lyne and Burnley.

Tintown. This nickname can be dated almost exactly. It was applied to an area of Rochdale, near the Rochdale Hornets ground, on which there were erected some "pre-fabs" in the 1940s. It is an example of an "area" nickname—see Prescot, Bury.

Rochdale Ruffyeds. Though commonly used in connection with Oldham people, this term was at one time applied to Rochdalians. Samuel Bamford, in "Earlydays" (Chapter 14) mentions this nickname. See Oldham.

Rochdale Puddings. Not a nickname, but a local foodstuff referred to in a poem—see Oldham. It gives added support to the belief that pig-keeping was common in Rochdale. **Rochdale Gawbies.** This nickname was applied to many townsfolk. It does not seem to have been widely applied to Rochdalians. See Shaw and others. **"In Rochdale, strangers prosper, natives fail."** This saying probably arose in Rochdale's early days as an industrial centre. I do not know how widely known it was. Similar sayings exist which relate to other towns.

Rochdale Hornets. The name of the town's Rugby League Club, which has been applied to the townsfolk generally in exactly the same way as football clubs elsewhere have lent their names to townsfolk. See Burnley, Chorley. The Hornets club was founded in 1871 from amalgamated clubs. The name can be dated exactly from 20th April, 1871. Other names suggested for the new club were "Wasps", "Butterflies" and "Grasshoppers".

Cowboyland. In the summer of 1975, the Lancashire folksinger/ entertainer Mike Harding recorded a nonsense song that he had written about a cowboy from Rochdale who rode a dog instead of a horse, and who wore spurs to do it. The song was a nation-wide success, and earned for him the nickname "The Rochdale Cowboy", which was the song's title. Even as late as the following year, a young Rochdale girl told me she was "from Cowboy-land". Daft I know, but this just shows how nicknames can be created, taken into use and perhaps their origin forgotten.

ROE GREEN, near Worsley

Teetotal Village. This nickname dates back to the time when the small village was particularly associated with the Total Abstinence movement, which was centred locally on the Independent Methodist Chapel. Throughout the years, local feeling has been strong enough to resist efforts to build or open a licensed house in the village, though in 1968 a Justices' Registration Certificate was granted to the Roe Green Cricket Club to enable liquor to be served and consumed there. See "Lancashire Life" magazine, October 1971. Another Lancashire village, Scorton (near Garstang), shares Roe Green's "dry" history, though Scorton has had no nickname.

ROSSENDALE VALLEY

Rossendale Clodhoppers, Rossendale Nutcrackers. Both these names are probably derived from the fame of Rossendalians for Morris dancing. In 1857 a troupe was formed called the Tunstead Mill Troupe, forerunners of the world-famous Britannia Coconut Dancers of which Bacup and the whole valley is so proud today. See the essay on them in "A Bacup Miscellany" by Kenneth F. Bowden (1972), but better still, go to Bacup on Easter Saturday and enjoy their dancing to that infectious music.

T'Golden Valley. A hundred years ago, the valley was vibrant with machinery. Mills made muck and that which follows it. In Bacup alone there were 67 cotton mills, so we can infer that the valley was golden because of the money earned there (not by everyone of course). Nevertheless, the valley's occupants were proud of the natural beauty existing before the Industrial Revolution, and may well have named it in such glowing terms to reflect their pride.

The Bathroom of England. No doubt so called because of the amount of rain showering down. It was coined by a person described by the editor of "Lancashire Life" as "a friend from a drier land".

ROYTON

Royton Wratchers. To wratch is the dialect expression meaning to stretch. The same story is told of Roytonians as occurs in Lees. **Royton Ranters** or **Royton Rants.** Primitive Methodists had the nickname "Ranters" applied to them in exactly the same way as members of the Society of Friends were called "Quakers". In fact, in the early days "Quakers" were called "Ranters". Primitive Methodism did not reach Royton until 1820, and ranting referred to the enthusiasm shown by the Primitive Methodists. The nickname had "died" by 1850. Though Royton is not thought to have been a particularly religious town, it is suggested that this religious connection is the reason for the nickname being applied. If so it is the only Lancashire example of a "religious" type of nickname.

Royton Sevens. Several reasons for this name being applied to the inhabitants can be found. Firstly, in the Civil War the local landowning Byron family showed active loyalty to the King. After he had been executed, Parliament passed an Act which "forgave" the late King's followers, but imposed a heavy fine. However, Byron's zeal had been so great and he was considered so dangerous that, along with six other people (thus making seven), he was denied clemency. Secondly, there were at one time seven mill owners in Royton who were described as "tight". They combined together so that, if one did not pay out to the demands of the workers, then neither did the other six.

Thirdly, there was a custom of youths in the town to parade up and down the streets seven abreast with locked arms on festive occasions. See LBY. A Royton man, the late Leigh Dunkerley, wrote a poem, probably not published, called "The Royton Seven".

SABDEN, near Whalley

Sabden Treacle Miners. The inhabitants of Sabden allegedly worked in the far-famed Sabden Treacle Mines. When these imaginary mines first became known to locals is not known, but they probably became known in much the same way as the "Higham Balloon Juice Company" which was floated — so to speak — by the "regulars" of the Four Alls Inn at Higham in the early 1930s. A prospectus and balance sheet were issued and considerable publicity resulted. Money raised in "Shares" benefited Burnley Victoria Hospital, and the "Burnley Express" newspaper at that time carried articles on company activities. The company's fame grew to such an extent that applications for shares were received from rational people all over the world. The comedian Ken Dodd tells of other treacle mines at Knotty Ash, Liverpool, and there were, indeed there still are, such mines at Tockholes, Blackburn.

SADDLEWORTH

Saddleworth is geographically in Lancashire and Yorkshire, and placed in Yorkshire for most administrative purposes, but since I see Ammon Wrigley as a Lancashire writer and Saddleworth folk no different from their neighbours to the west, I have included it in this book.

Saddleworth Tykes. As everyone knows, a Tyke is a Yorkshireman, and this name was undoubtedly given by someone from the Lancashire side of the Pennines, probably Oldham, to allude to the affinity between Saddleworth and Yorkshire.

Saddleworth Gloves. Not a nickname at all, but a phrase dreamed up by Ammon Wrigley to describe pockets. If a man was wearing Saddleworth gloves, he had his hands in his pockets, and needed to have them there to protect him from the wind blowing over the heather on Saddleworth moors. It reminds me of "a Bacup look"—with one's hands.

"Like the parson of Saddleworth, who could read no book but his own." Bridge records this being used in Cheshire in 1670. There is no such Cheshire place, but it is interesting to remember that Saddleworth was in the Diocese of Chester at one time, though Bridge regards the name as being fictitious in that it could have been any township used in the phrase, as the saying was without foundation. Ammon Wrigley, the Saddleworth storyteller, would have told us.

SALFORD

Salford Doffers. Salford can probably be said to have risen in stature because of the cotton industry. Doffers were mill workers, mostly young lads, whose job was to "doff" or remove the full bobbins from the spinning frames and replace them with empty ones. They were usually very mischievous because they had a lot of free time provided that they kept production up. A spinner or weaver must never be "stuck for bobbins". **Salford Lads**, see Liverpool.

SCHOLES, Wigan

Scholes is locally pronounced **"Scowze"**. It is in fact derived from "school". The local grammar school was built in 1597. It makes one wonder whether grammar was taught. **Scowlers.** The inhabitants of Scholes (Scowles). **Scoze Woppers.** A wopper, or whopper, is universally known as a large thing. Past generations of Scholes men worked in heavy industries such as iron works, coal mines and quarries. They were large in stature and strength, with thirsts, appetites and hearts to match. Their womenfolk were equally prodigious, and it was mainly to these lasses that the term was applied.

Edwin Waugh described a visit made to Scholes in which he went to "a dirty square called **'The Coal Yard'** ". This would be some local nickname derived from the town's staple trade.

SHARNEYFORD, near Bacup

Sharneyford Tups. A "tup" is the dialect word, still in common use among farmers, for a ram. Sharneyford is a hillside hamlet where sheep have long been reared, so the name may have this connection. Also it may be spiced with humour of the pun to suggest that Sharneyford men were as noted for their sexual prowess as is the ram.

SHAW, near Oldham

Shaw is locally pronounced **"Shay"**.
Shaw Gawbies or Gorbies. A "gawby" is an idiot or simpleton: See EDD. It was in common use up to the 1920s at least. The locals take some pride in the nickname, and tell several stories to illustrate the gawmlessness of their ancestors. One is that a man went round Shaw selling tickets to people who could then watch a mill chimney being painted white. As this was unusual he sold a lot of tickets. The "gawbies" stood watching for some time before realising they had been "sowd a pup", then they went round Shaw "gawping" or looking for him.

Shaw Chimney Droppers. This nickname arose after a man was supposed to have invented an inflatable suit to save steeplejacks being killed if they fell off a chimney. When it was used, the story goes, the man kept on bouncing until he had to be shot down. I am struck by the idea that the Shaw folk could not be stupid at all if they could think up stories like this one.

Shaw Shaftwratchers. This story too is connected with gawm-lessness: See Lees and Rochdale. Shaw is called **"The Desert"** by Oldham folk, because it is said, "there's nowt theer."

SHOLVER, Oldham

Sholver Pullets, or in the dialect **Showver Poots.** This nickname may have arisen out of the simplicity of the local people and the prevalence of moorhens there, but it may be compared with "Northmoor Goslings" and it may be wondered whether one name was not chosen from a domestic fowl to counter the other.

SKELMERSDALE

Skem. The name was corrupted (shortened, us Lancastrians say) to this convenient word, in just the same way as Oswaldtwistle became "Ozzy".

T'Skem Jazzer. This was a steam train running on the local line. I haven't been able to find a date when the name came into use, but it was probably during the Jazz Age—the Twenties. The line was closed to passenger traffic in 1956.

SMALLBRIDGE, Rochdale

The name is properly pronounced **"Smo'brig"** or **"Smo'bridge"**— FET.

Smallbridge Sand Knockers. In the earlier edition, I suggested that this name was derived from the knockers-up who toured the area in the early hours of each working day, knocking on windows with bags of sand. More research has brought to light a much more sensible origin of the name. Local writer Edwin Waugh, in his "Lancashire Sketches", describes the folk as:— "A race of hereditary sand-sellers, or 'sond-knockers',—a rough mountain breed who live by crushing sandstone rocks for sale in the town of Rochdale and the villages about it. The sand is used for strewing on the flagged house floors when the floor is clean washed; and while it is yet damp the sand is ground over it by the motion of a heavy scouring stone ... the motion of the stone grinds the sand into smoothness, and leaves an ornamental whiteness on the floor when it gets dry. ... The people who knock this sand and sell it have been known over the countryside for many years (he wrote about 1870) by the name of **'T' Kitters'** and the common local proverb **'We're o' ov a litter, like Kitter pigs'** is used in Smallbridge as an expression of friendship or kinship." FET adds that **Smallbridge Kitters** was a local name for Smallbridge folk. The Sand Knocker tradition has been permanently recorded in the name of a pub locally. In the township was a Kitter Street, a Kitter Square, and a Sand Street.

Smallbridge Cossacks. Said to be a sarcastic name for the inhabitants—FET. It was difficult to suggest an origin for the name until an old resident told me that he believed it came from the trading sand-knockers who were to be seen, with their horses and carts, conducting themselves in a noisy manner in some local pub after selling their wares. However, see the explanation for the same Whitefield name.

SOUTHPORT

Sandgrounders. In common with nicknames applied to other parts of Lancashire's coast, this one alludes to the sand of the coast: See Blackpool, Lytham St. Annes, Morecambe. Two local history books give space to discuss the matter of being a true "sandgrounder", and I quote from them:—

"Sunny Southport, 1903: Sandgrounder". In the local vernacular, a " 'sandgrounder' is one born in Southport of parents who were themselves born there; but it is a common saying that if a man remains long in the town until he 'gets sand in his shoes', he becomes a 'Sandgrounder'. The soil of Southport is, as everyone knows, of a very sandy nature—hence 'Sandgrounder' or 'Son of the soil'."

"History of Southport", F. A. Bailey, 1955: "Properly speaking, according to old legends," said Bland, "a Sandgrounder must be born on sand land betwixt Alt and Astland. There is still some conflict of opinion as to how many generations of settlement are necessary to qualify for the assumption of this valued title. This nickname is almost certainly older than the 'sand grown' of Blackpool and Lytham St. Annes, as it was mainly by Southport fishing families that those townships were first populated."

Montpelier of the North. This delightful phrase was found in a Blackpool newspaper of 1876. It was possibly a name given to the town by its own inhabitants, but in the newspaper was used scurrilously in an article attacking Southport's sewerage facilities, or lack of them.

England's Seaside Garden City. A term used by the town's Publicity Department in the 1937 Holiday Brochure.

Little Ireland. In common with other Lancashire towns, Southport has an area which was at one time known as "Little Ireland". The Marsh Side area of the town was favoured by the early Irish immigrants, and the existing residents of the town gave the area this nickname, just as happened in Gaythorn and elsewhere.

The Southport football club team has acquired the nickname **"The Sandgrounders".**

ST. HELENS

The Saints, or simply **Saints.** This nickname does not appear to have been in use until comparatively recent times, and was popularised by the success of the town rugby team. It is an example of a nickname developing from a sports team name to a general name applied to townsfolk: See Burnley, Chorley. The rugby club has adopted the song: "When the Saints go marching in" as its song.

Chemics. The chemical industry is the major industry in the town, and has been for many years. This nickname, also applied to a lesser degree to the rugby team, is a reference to the industry.

STANDISH, near Wigan

Standish Pow-yeds. A "pow" is the dialect expression for "haircut". The nickname is simply a derogatory term. Its modern equivalent is "skin-head" for the short haircut style.

STOCKPORT

"Eyup, what's Stockport doing here?" I hear you say. Stockport was at one time partly in Lancashire, partly in Cheshire, and thus qualifies for inclusion.

"When the world was made, the rubbish was sent to Stockport." Happily, not a much-used saying, but a phrase used in a novel "The Lady Shakerley" by Frances M. Wilbraham.

Stopport Law; no stake, no draw. Also used as "Lancashire Law" this phrase means that only those who contribute to an undertaking can reap the benefit, or simply put—"If you want a share in owt, you mun pay fer it." Bridge records the use of the saying in 1678.

STRETFORD

Porkhampton. The town of Stretford was formerly connected with pigs so strongly that all the town and townsfolk nicknames have some allusion to the pig trade. Pork butchers are mentioned in local registers in the mid-18th century. It is said that thousands of pigs would arrive at Stretford at a time, the main streets being blocked by them. Householders moved furniture out of their parlours to make room for bacon and ham salting and curing, which used to take two or three months. Pig carcases were distributed from Stretford all over Lancashire and Yorkshire.

The other nicknames traced are: **Stretford Black Puddings** for the inhabitants; **Boudin Noir,** which is French for black pudding; **Stretford Goose**—a local name for roast pork stuffed with sage and onions (the poor man's goose)—FET; **Rhubarb Town; and Black Pudding Junction.** See Bury; and see Crofton, "History of Ancient Chapel of Stretford", vol. 3 (Chetham Society 1903).

SUNDERLAND POINT, near Heysham

Cape Famine. This nickname was given to Sunderland Point by sailors who were anchored off the mouth of the Lune while their ship's cargo was being lightered up river to Lancaster. There was no form of amusement for sailors there, only fishermen's cottages. There were not even any public houses or social events for the crews' enjoyment. It remains today very much as it has always been.

THATTO HEATH, St. Helens

Donkey Commoners. In Thatto Heath there is a green, or common, and at one time donkeys were kept there for children's rides, in exactly the same way as donkeys are kept on the beaches of Lancashire holiday resorts.

TOTTINGTON, near Bury

Pig o't'Wall. The story has long been told that the gawmless folk of Tottington, a sleepy village, put their pigs up on to a wall so that the dear things could watch the passing of any band or procession. The same story is told of the folk of other Lancashire villages, but the name seems to be associated more strongly with Tottington than with the other places, perhaps through the efforts of Tommy Thompson, a well known Lancashire story-teller who wrote a great deal, both books of his own and articles in the "Manchester Guardian". He broadcast, too, and though he does not mention the story often in his books, I believe that his connection with Tottington—he lived there for many years—has helped to popularise the village and the story.

TRAWDEN, near Colne

"**Trawden, where the ace of trumps did not take a trick.**" Said by local writer Weeks to be a local saying, but one that I can't yet explain.

TYLDESLEY

Tyldesley is known as **"Bongs". Tyldesley Bongs or Bonks.** Tyldesley is built on banks, or steep hills. The low land to the rising banks is the termination of the level plain which starts at Irlam, embraces Chat Moss and Astley Moss and is five miles across. See Crawshawbooth; and see SWP.

UNSWORTH, part of Bury

Gawbyshire, a jocular name for Unsworth village—FET; see Shaw.
T'Numb City. Apparently, in the last century, Unsworth folk had a reputation for foolish tricks. The name adds strength to the argument that the folk there were "gawbies". **Unsworth pig o'th' wallers.** Yet another village to which the story of the pig on the wall to watch the band go by is said to apply. It again illustrates the villagers' gawmlessness. See Tottington.
   Unsworth Dragon. This is not a nickname. There is a tradition that Thomas Unsworth, the local squire, killed a dragon which was attacking villagers. See LL and Hird. A pub in which the dragon appears on the signboard has recently been opened in the village.

WARRINGTON

Warrington Wires, or Wirepullers. The craft of wirepulling was practised in Warrington in the 19th century and the town has strong connections with the wire industry. The town rugby club was at one time nicknamed **"T' wirepullers"**, now shortened to **"T' wires".** The name is mostly now used in connection with the rugby team.

Warrington—the **Athens of England.** In the 18th century, the Warrington Dissenting Academy was a famous centre of education, and many eminent scholars, writers and craftsmen were educated or taught there. It became a leading educational establishment, and thus Warrington became likened to Athens, the centre of learning of the ancient world. A lecture on this subject was given to the Lancashire and Cheshire Antiquarian Society in 1926 by Arthur Bennett, a Warrington historian, and it was reprinted in the "Warrington Examiner" in 1927.

WARTON, near Carnforth

Treacle Lane. A bridleway leading from the Borwick road not far from Warton village has been known as Treacle Lane for many years. Not many know that its true name is Three Gill (hard "g") Lane, and that Treacle is a contraction.

Paint Mines. Some 19th century iron-ore mine workings on the north-west side of Warton Crag are now deserted and nature is taking over again. The earth there is red through natural minerals colouring it. A red pigment was used in paint making, and thus the name arose, inferring that paint itself was mined there.

WARTON, near Kirkham

Little America. In the Second World War there was an American air base at the Warton airfield now used by the British Aircraft Corporation. There were many Yanks stationed there, and they brightened the old place up somewhat. I wouldn't be surprised to find that Warrington was so called too, when the Burtonwood Air Base was in full swing.

WATERFOOT, Rossendale

Waterfoot Sad-Cakers. This nickname was applied because of the reputed fancy of the people for sad cake with jam on. See Lumb in Rossendale, and Weir. The poem in Digby's "Rossendale Anthology" (p. 123) refers to Waterfoot folk preferring sad cake to trout.

WEASTE, Salford

Weaste Puppies. This is "the uncomplimentary byname of dwellers in this suburb of Manchester"—LBY. There seems to be no reason for the name, except that it was intended as a derogatory nickname.

WEIR, Rossendale

Jamland. It seems quite natural that "Jamland" should be near "Sad Cake Land": See Waterfoot, and a poem written by a Weir lady in Digby's "Rossendale Anthology", p. 123. There was a time within living memory when families were sustained for long periods on "jam butties", a cheap food.

WESTHOUGHTON, near Bolton

Westhoughton Keawyeds. This nickname is given in the local dialect. It means "Cow Heads". The town itself is referred to as **"Keawyed City"** or simply **"Keawyed"**. The nickname is in regular use today. Legend tells of a Westhoughton farmer seeing that a cow had its head "stuck fast in a gate", and to free it he simply cut off the cow's head. A Westhoughton poet, Ernie Ford, has written a poem to illustrate the legend in the dialect of the town. It is called "Howfen Legend", and **"Howfen"** is another local dialect name for the town, a contraction of Westhoughton.

A stained glass window in the Waggon and Horses Hotel, Westhoughton, depicts the scene, which is often enacted in playful manner in local public houses at the time of the annual fair. The fair is called the "pasty eating wakes" because of the liking of locals for this food many years ago, but it was really initiated to celebrate the feast of St. Bartholomew. See Harrison T., "Britain revisited", 1961.

WHALLEY

Abbeyites. This nickname was coined about the turn of the century by a sports reporter who was referring to the town cricket team. It is still used in this context, and alludes to Whalley Abbey.

"Madhouse Farm". The farmstead properly called Mitton Fold Farm, near Whalley, was from the mid-19th century connected with the Langho lunatic asylum, and thus it was nicknamed "Madhouse Farm".

"The proud wives of Whalley". Thus did Harrison Ainsworth describe the ladies of Read Hall, near Whalley, in his "Lancashire Witches".

The ecclesiastical parish of Whalley was the largest in the county at the beginning of the 19th century. It occupied a ninth of the county.

WHITEFIELD

Whitefield — **Whitfield** in the dialect. **Whitefield Dobbers.** A jocular name for the inhabitants of Whitefield—FET. The nickname of "dobber" is almost certainly connected with the textile industry, long associated with Whitefield, although weaving and spinning gave way to bleaching and dyeing some years ago as the town's major industries. A dobber would be a person who controlled a dobby loom. In layman's terms, a dobby, or dobbie, is an attachment fixed on to a loom for devising a simple pattern. The first reference to a dobbie was in 1878, so this will help to date the nickname.

In Whitefield is an area called Park Lane, and on p. 40 of his book "Pilkington Park", Thomas Holt recalls a rhyme:

> *Park Lane dobbers has no sense,*
> *Worked in a factory for eighteenpence.*
> *Eighteenpence would never do*
> *To keep a wife and family too.*

FET defines "dobber" as (a) large marble and (b) a float on an angler's line. I think the present equivalent is "bobber".
Park Lane Cossacks. At the time of the Crimean War, the inhabitants of the Park Lane area of Whitefield were given this name. It stuck, and in time only those born in the area were Cossacks, the rest foreigners. See Smallbridge.
Little Ireland. One area of Whitefield was at some time known by this nickname. I quote from Holt's book "Pilkington Park": "In direct contrast to the beauties of Hollinhurst, and on its doorstep as it were, was the district known as 'Little Ireland', a mean collection of houses with little sanitation, peopled mostly by those of an improvident nature, with little thought for tomorrow." Their ways are said to have improved after the passing of the Truck Act, but I suspect that the name would continue in use into this century, at least up to the First World War. See Gaythorn; and see Schofield, "Reminiscences of Whitefield", 1822.

WHITTLE-LE-WOODS, near Chorley

Whittle Crows. LBY reasons that this nickname arose because of a large wood near the hamlet with a large rookery in it.

WHITWORTH, near Rochdale

In the local pronunciation—**Whit'oth. Whitworth "Doctors".** This is not a nickname applied to anyone, but a collective name applied to a famous family of doctors called Taylor. The family, headed by John Taylor—he came to the notice of King George III—practised in Whitworth and had a shop at Rochdale where patients and their animals could attend to be cured of cancers and broken limbs. Their fame was widespread and they were consulted by lords and commoners. See "The Palatine Notebook" 1882, "Rochdale Observer" 1876, Digby and Bowden, "Bacup Miscellany", 1972.

WIDNES

Chemics. This nickname, coined to be applied to the town rugby team, is sometimes applied to the townsfolk. It arises from the local chemical industry. See St. Helens. FET gives: Chemics—chemical bodies used in the manufacture of anything, pronounced "kimmicks".

WIGAN

Wigan is locally pronounced **"Wiggin". Wiggin Hearty-Christers.** This is intended as a jocular nickname. Years ago, Wiganers had a reputation for wickedness. John Wesley noted that Wigan was "proverbially famed for all manner of wickedness"; but 25 years after his first visit he said: "It is now not what it was. The inhabitants have taken a softer mould." See Ormerod, "Lancashire Life and Character", p. 172. The name alludes to a form of oath peculiar to the place, especially amongst the colliers: "Bi' th' hearty Christ", or "By the heart of Christ".—FET. It bears a good deal of similarity to the oaths once common in Lancashire: "Bi' t' Mass" and "Bi' t' Mon", which means "By the Mass" and "By the God, or Jesus".

Wigan Mop Rags. Probably simply a derogatory nickname.—LBY.

Wigan Purrers. Purring means kicking, and kicking matches amongst the colliers were common, resulting in broken limbs from clog-toes: See Pendlebury. **T'Colliers** and **T'Pitmen.** These terms, applied generally to Wiganers, are often applied to the Wigan Rugby Club and Wigan Athletic Football Club teams. Wigan was the centre of the Lancashire coalfield and the capital of the coal industry in Lancashire.

Wigan Alps. Wigan is still associated in the minds of Lancashire people with coalpits and slag heaps. It was those slag heaps, towering above the ground level, and easily seen from roadway or railway nearby, which looked like mountains and so they were named—The Alps. They were, indeed still are in many cases, found alongside what Wiganers call "flashes", that is lodges of water pumped out of the pits. These were found to some degree all over the area, but specially to the south east, where early

O.S. maps record in blue the expanses of water called Scotsman's Flash, Pearson's Flash and Anderton's Flash. I quote a delightful phrase from a book by J. J. Bagley, "Lancashire": "To the East of Wigan, the resultant hollows, the flashes, and the steep sierras of industrial waste have earned the ironical nickname of **The Lake District** and **The Wigan Alps**."

T'Lump. A village on the outskirts of Wigan, Bryn Gates has long been called **"Lump"** or **"T'owd Lump"** by locals. It was so named on the 1892 O.S. map, showing it to be on the east of Bolton Road, close to the houses there, and near to the sewerage works of Ashton-in-Makerfield Council. It has been suggested that the name was one having some connection with the slag heaps, but I discount this, as there were no heaps there when the name was first used. Was the place hilly? No, though there is a hill to the south, nearer Ashton-in-Makerfield. I think it may have been named because it stuck out, as does a lump, boil or sore, from the open expanse of the surrounding countryside. The village lies about halfway between Ashton-in-Makerfield and Platt Bridge, close to Bamfurlong. The word "lump" appears too in "Cock's Lump" which is between Bryn and Worsley Mesnes on Wigan Road.

The Three Sisters were three monstrous slag heaps, said to be about 160 feet high at their highest point, which stood in Ashton-in-Makerfield and took slag from Bamfurlong Colliery and Smethurst Collieries. They were levelled in the early 1970s, and a small hillock is all that remains of them, as the area has been landscaped to become grazing land again. Locally, such heaps were known as "rooks", "dirt rooks" or "shale rooks". Those known as "ash rooks" were composed of ashes taken from colliery boilers. I have heard of some such heaps being called **"The Seven Sisters"** but haven't been able to pinpoint them or verify their number.

WINWICK, near Warrington

Winwick Pig o'th' Wallers. The traditional story of the simpleton putting his pig up to a wall to watch the band or procession pass is told about many Lancashire towns: See Tottington. However, this nickname has a different meaning when applied to Winwick folk.

According to tradition, the stones used in the building of St. Oswald's Church, Winwick, were moved nightly to their present site after being first built on another site. Apparently the pig wished the church to be on this particular site. It is a tradition repeated at Rochdale, Burnley and Samlesbury and also places outside Lancashire. St. Oswald's varies from these other churches in that the stonemasons who built the tower incorporated into the west wall an effigy of a pig with a bell chained round his neck. This has become the Winwick mascot. One explanation offered for the masons' work is that it is their way of putting the initials of the church on the church itself — St. Oswald's Winwick (S.O.W.).

Another traditional story connects Winwick with the pig. It goes that a pig was seen round the new church, St. Oswald's, crying "Wee-wick, wee-wick". The pig carried a stone in its mouth to a nearby site where St. Oswald was killed and the church was built there. It is a slight variation on the "pig in the night" story.

Bibliography

(Books referred to by abbreviation or author in the text.)

LBY   "Lancashire Town Bynames", F. J. Irwin, S.J., in the "Stonyhurst Magazine" 1928.

LL   "Lancashire Legends", Harland & Wilkinson, 1882.

Hird   "Lancashire Stories", Frank Hird, undated.

ABSL   "Ancient Ballads & Songs of Lancashire", Harland & Wilkinson, 1875.

FET   "The Folk-Speech of South-East Lancashire", F. E. Taylor, 1901.

EDD   "English Dialect Dictionary", J. Wright (6 vols.).

SWP   "Place Proverbs & Rhymes", S. W. Partington, 1910.

VCH   "Victoria County History of Lancashire", 1908.

Blakey   "Annals & Stories of Barrowford", Jesse Blakey, 1929.

Carr   "Annals & Stories of Colne & Neighbourhood", James Carr, 1878.

Bridge   "Cheshire Proverbs & Other Sayings & Rhymes" J. Bridge, 1917.

Thornber   "An historical & descriptive account of Blackpool & neighbourhood", Wm. Thornber, 1837.